Darwin and Intelligent Design

FACETS

Selected Titles in the Facets Series

Darwin
and
Intelligent Design

Francisco J. Ayala

Fortress Press
Minneapolis

DARWIN AND INTELLIGENT DESIGN

Cover image: © Clouds Hill Imaging Ltd./Corbis
Book design: Joseph P. Bonyata

Library of Congress Cataloging-in-Publication Data

Ayala, Francisco José, 1934-
  Darwin and intelligent design / Francisco J. Ayala.
       p. cm. — (Facets)
  Includes bibliographical references.
  ISBN-13: 978-0-8006-3802-3 (alk. paper)
  ISBN-10: 0-8006-3802-6
  1. Religion and science. 2. Evolution (Biology)—Religious aspects—Christianity. 3. Evolution (Biology) 4. Intelligent design (Teleology) 5. Darwin, Charles, 1809-1882. I. Title.
  BL263.A93 2006
  231.7'652—dc22

                                          2006021348

The paper used in this publication meets the minimum requirements of American National Standard for Information Sciences—Permanence of Paper for Printed Library Materials, ANSI Z329.48-1984.

Manufactured in the U.S.A.

10 09 08 07 06   2   3   4   5   6   7   8   9   10

Contents

Prologue

The message that this little book seeks to convey is that science and religious beliefs need not be in contradiction. This message has a long Christian tradition that extends since the time of Augustine in the fourth century, and even earlier, to Pope John Paul II and other religious authorities of the present. There are many believers in the United States and elsewhere who think that science, particularly the theory of evolution, is contrary to the teachings of the Bible and to religious beliefs, such as Creation by God. Science has demonstrated again and again, beyond reasonable doubt, that living organisms evolve and diversify over time, and that their features have come about by natural selection, a process that accounts for their "design." I will seek to convince you, dear reader, that we may accept this scientific knowledge without denying the existence of God or God's presence in the universe and all natural phenomena. Science can neither endorse nor reject religious beliefs. Conversely, we should not interpret the Bible as an authoritative textbook on astronomy, geology, or biology.

Thomas Aquinas (1224–1274), following a long Christian tradition that extends back at least to Augustine (354–430), distinguished two sources of knowledge: reason and divine revelation. The incarnation and the trinity are theological truths that can only be known through revelation. By means of experience and logical reasoning, human beings can acquire valid knowledge and construct a science of the natural world. In public disputations at the University of Paris, Thomas famously argued that rational truth and revelation cannot be incompatible. Contradictions can only be apparent as a result of erroneous interpretation of Scripture or faulty reasoning.

According to Augustine, in his commentary on the book of Genesis, Christians should not seek to settle scientific matters with sacred Scripture: "Such subjects are of no profit for those who seek beatitude. . . . In the matter of the shape of heaven, the sacred writers did not wish to teach men facts that could be of no avail for their salvation." Augustine added: "If it happens that the authority of Sacred Scripture is set in opposition to clear and certain reasoning, this must mean that the person who interprets Scripture does not understand it correctly."

Similarly, Pope John Paul II wrote: "The Bible itself speaks to us of the origin of the universe and its make-up, not in order to provide us with a scientific treatise but in order to state the correct relationships of man with God and the universe." Moreover, "sacred Scripture wishes simply to declare that the world was created by God, and in order to teach this truth it expresses itself *in the terms of the cosmology in use at the time of the writer*" (emphasis added).

My message is the same as those of Augustine, Thomas Aquinas, and Pope John Paul: science and religion are compatible. I will focus on the theory of evolution by natural selection, first proposed by Charles Darwin, which I will explain the best I can within the confines of this short book. It may surprise you, dear reader, but I will argue that evolution is more compatible with Christianity than "intelligent design" and other creationist theories.

In chapter 1 I situate my argument by noting that the notion of intelligent design has a long history in Christianity, from Augustine through Thomas Aquinas to William Paley, who at the start of the nineteenth century argued that the eye and other adaptive features of organisms evince that they have been designed by an omniscient Creator.

I introduce Charles Darwin in chapter 2, highlighting Darwin's discovery of natural selection as a scientific explanation of the design of organisms, just as gravity and other discoveries of Newtonian mechanics had explained the revolutions of the earth and planets around the sun.

Evolutionary theories are old (chapter 3), but only after Darwin's discovery of natural selection did it become possible to explain how evolution occurs. The evidence for evolution is overwhelming; it has accumulated at an increasing rate since Darwin's time.

Chapter 4 summarizes human evolution: thousands of fossil intermediates ("missing links") between apes and humans have been discovered. Our ancestors of six million years ago were bipedal but had a small brain, which became larger over time.

I explain natural selection in chapter 5. My main purpose is to show that natural selection accounts for the adaptation of organisms to their environments (their design). The process of natural selection explains why organisms change over eons of time and diversify as they adapt to environments that are enormously diverse.

William Paley's argument from design was revived in the 1990s (without any reference to Paley), starting the intelligent design (ID) movement (chapter 6). The evidence and arguments of ID proponents are bad science; they have no scientific cogency whatsoever. Moreover, ID is bad religion. The design of organisms is not intelligent, but imperfect and riddled with dysfunctionalities; ID implies attributes of God that are incompatible with Christianity and other monotheistic religions.

The final chapter completes my argument by drawing out the important conclusion that evolution (more generally, science) is not incompatible with religion. Indeed, science and religion *cannot* be incompatible, because they concern nonoverlapping domains of knowledge. I add that science is a very successful way of acquiring knowledge, but it is not the only way. We acquire knowledge about the nature of the world, about values, and about the meaning and purpose of life and the universe from literature, art, philosophy, and religion.

Federal judge John E. Jones III wrote, in the *Dover* decision of December 20, 2005, that "the leading proponents of ID make a bedrock assumption which is utterly false. Their presupposition is that evolutionary theory is antithetical to a belief in the existence of a supreme being and to religion in general."

The popularity of the ID movement is not because it is good science—it definitely is not—nor because it bolsters religious beliefs, which it also fails to do. Rather, I see ID as a nostrum: it falsely presents itself under the guise of scientific support for the existence of God, making ID readily accepted by people of good will who treasure their religious beliefs. My message is this: believers should seek support in their faith, not in spurious scientific arguments.

William Paley

Christianity, Judaism, Islam, and other monotheistic religions explain the origin of the
universe, the earth, and all living beings as the
handiwork of an omnipotent and omniscient God.
Since the early times of Christianity, religious
authors have explained that the orderly design of
the universe is evidence of the existence of God.
Thus, Augustine affirmed that "the world itself, by
the perfect order of its changes and motions and by
the great beauty of all things visible, proclaims . . .
that it has been created, and also that it could not
have been made other than by a God ineffable and
invisible in greatness, and . . . in beauty."[1]

The great theologian Thomas Aquinas distinguished between truths, such as the incarnation
and the trinity, that can be known only by divine
revelation, and truths accessible by human reason, which include God's existence. God's existence can be demonstrated in five different ways.
Thomas's "fifth way" is based on the harmonious
design of the universe, which can only come from

"some entity endowed with knowledge and intelligence. . . . Therefore some intelligent being exists by which all natural things are directed to their end; and this being we call God."[2]

John Ray (1627–1705), an English clergyman and naturalist, dedicated a full book to the argument that all components of the universe—the stars and the planets as well as all living beings—are so wisely contrived from the beginning and so perfect in their operation that they provide incontrovertible evidence of God's wisdom. In *The Wisdom of God Manifested in the Works of Creation* (1691), Ray writes that the "most convincing argument of the existence of a deity is the admirable Art and Wisdom that discovers itself in the Make of the Constitution, the Order and Disposition, the Ends and uses of all parts and members of this stately fabric of Heaven and Earth."[3]

Argument from Design

The most extensive, authoritative, and beautifully written argument from design was written by the English clergyman William Paley (1743–1805). Paley was intensely committed to the abolition of the slave trade and had become by the 1780s a much-sought public speaker against slavery. He was also an influential writer of works on Christian philosophy, ethics, and theology. *The Principles of Moral and Political Philosophy* (1785) and *A View of the Evidence of Christianity* (1794) earned him prestige and well-endowed ecclesiastical benefices, which allowed him a comfortable life. Illness forced him in 1800 to give up his public speaking career, which provided him with ample time to study science, particularly biology, and write *Natural Theology; or, Evidences of the Existence and Attributes of the Deity* (1802), the book by which he has become best known to posterity and which would greatly influence Darwin.

Paley sought to update John Ray's *Wisdom of God Manifested in the Works of the Creation*, taking advantage of one century of additional scientific knowledge. *Natural Theology* is a sustained argument inferring the existence of God from the obvious design of humans and their organs, as well as the design of all sorts of organisms, in themselves and in their relations to one another and to their environment. The argument has two parts: first, that organisms give evidence of being designed; second, only an omnipotent God could account for the perfection, multitude, and diversity of the design.

There are chapters dedicated to the complex design of the human eye; to the human frame, which displays a precise mechanical arrangement of bones, cartilage, and joints; to the circulation of the blood and the disposition of blood vessels; to the comparative anatomy of humans and animals; to the digestive tract, kidneys, urethras, and bladder; to the wings of birds and the fins of fish; and much more. For 352 pages *Natural Theology* conveys Paley's expertise: extensive and accurate biological knowledge, as detailed and precise as was available in the year 1800. After detailing the specific organization and exquisite functionality of each biological entity or process, Paley draws again and again the same conclusion: that only an omniscient and omnipotent deity could account for these marvels of mechanical perfection, purpose, and functionality, and for the enormous diversity of inventions that they entail.

Paley's first model example is the human eye, in chapter 3:

> I know no better method of introducing so large a subject, than that of comparing a single thing with a single thing: an eye, for example, with a telescope. . . . There is precisely the same proof that the eye was made for vision, as there is that the telescope was made for assisting it. They are made upon the same principles; both being adjusted to the laws by which the transmission and refraction of rays of light are regulated.[4]

Paley summarizes his argument by stating the complex functional anatomy of the eye:

> [We marvel] knowing as we do what an eye comprehends, namely, that it should have consisted, first, of a series of transparent lenses—very different, by the by, even in their substance, from the opaque materials of which the rest of the body is, in general at least, composed, . . . secondly, of a black cloth or canvas [the retina] . . . spread out behind these lenses, so as to receive the image

formed by pencils of light transmitted through them . . . thirdly, of a large nerve communicating between this membrane and the brain; without which, the action of light upon the membrane, however modified by the organ, would be lost to the purposes of sensation.[5]

Paley marvels that the retina, "the only membrane of the body which is black," should be "placed at the precise geometrical distance at which, and at which alone, a distinct image could be formed, namely, at the concourse of the refracted rays."[6]

Could the eye have come about without design or preconceived purpose, as a result of chance? Paley had set the argument against chance in the very first paragraph of *Natural Theology*, arguing rhetorically by analogy:

In crossing a heath, suppose I pitched my foot against a *stone*, and were asked how the stone came to be there, I might possibly answer, that for any thing I knew to the contrary it had lain there for ever. . . . But suppose I had found a *watch* upon the ground, and it should be inquired how the watch happened to be in that place, I should hardly think of the answer which I had before given, that for any thing I knew the watch might have always been there."[7]

The reason, Paley says, is because the watch consists of many parts all designed to serve one precise function. "When we come to inspect the watch, we perceive—what we could not discover in the stone—that its several parts are framed and put together for a purpose, *e.g.* that they are so formed and adjusted as to produce motion, and that motion so regulated as to point out the hour of the day."[8]

The strength of the argument against chance derives, Paley tells us, from what he names "relation," a notion akin to what some contemporary authors have named "irreducible complexity." This is how Paley formulates the argument:

> When several different parts contribute to one effect, or, which is the same thing, when an effect is produced by the joint action of different instruments, the fitness of such parts or instruments to one another for the purpose of producing, by their united action, the effect, is what I call *relation*; and wherever this is observed in the works of nature or of man, it appears to me to carry along with it decisive evidence of understanding, intention, art.[9]

The outcomes of chance do not exhibit relation among the parts or, as we might say, organized complexity.

Paley displays extensive and profound biological knowledge. He discusses the air-bladder of fish, the fang of vipers, the claw of herons, the camel's stomach, the woodpecker's tongue, the elephant's proboscis, the hook in the bat's wing, the spider's web, the compound eyes of insects and their metamorphosis, the glowworm, univalve and bivalve mollusks, seed dispersal, and on and on, with accuracy and as much detail as known to the best biologists of his time. The organized complexity and purposeful function evince, in each case, intelligent design, and the diversity, richness, and pervasiveness of the designs evince that only an omnipotent Creator could be the intelligent designer.

The design of organisms and their complexity, the multiplicity of species and their interactions, set "the natural attributes of the Deity", namely, omnipotence, omniscience, omnipresence, eternity, self-existence, necessary existence, and spirituality.

Imperfections and Dysfunctions

Paley knows that he has to face two difficult issues: (1) organs or parts that seemingly are unnecessary or superfluous, and (2) organs that are imperfect and even dysfunctional.

There are two possible explanations for the occurrence of seemingly superfluous organs. In some cases, we are ignorant of the function of the organ, although we know that the organ is necessary for survival; in other cases, we are ignorant of whether the organ is used at all. Examples of the first kind include the lungs of animals, which Paley knew to be necessary for survival, although he was not "acquainted with the action of the air upon the blood, or in what manner that action is communicated by the lungs." He cites the lymphatic system as a second example of this kind. Instances "may be numerous; for they will be so in proportion to our ignorance. . . . Every improvement of knowledge diminishes their number." Examples of organs with unknown use include the spleen, which seems not to be necessary, for "it has been extracted from dogs without any sensible injury to their vital functions."[10] But it may well be the case that the part serves some unknown function, even if not necessary for survival in the short run.

This is Paley's general explanation of nature's imperfections: "Irregularities and imperfections are of little or no weight . . . but they are to be taken in conjunction with the unexceptionable evidences which we possess of skill, power, and benevolence displayed in other instances."[11] But this account is unconvincing. If functional design manifests an intelligent designer, why should not deficiencies indicate that the designer is less than omniscient, or less than omnipotent, or less than omnificent? Paley cannot have it both ways.

We know that some deficiencies are not just imperfections, but they are outright dysfunctional, jeopardizing the very function the organ or part is supposed to serve. Moreover, carnivorous predators behave in ways that by human standards would be judged cruel, and parasites seem designed with a sadistic purpose, since they exist by harming other organisms. The mating interactions between male and female in some insects, spiders, and other organisms would also be judged cruel and even sadistic by human standards. These are matters to which I shall return later.

Paley is honest enough to acknowledge the difficulties as he knew them. But his explanation is inconsistent with his overall argument. Even if the dysfunctions, cruelties, and sadism of the living world were rare, which they are not, they would still need to be attributed to the Designer if the Designer had designed the living world. The design of organisms is far from perfect. This is as we should expect from the process of natural selection. Darwin's theory provides the explanation of Paley's conundrum, as I shall explain in a following chapter.

After Paley

Natural theology was disfavored by the Reformation. Martin Luther and John Calvin denied that human nature, corrupted after the Fall, would have the power, without revelation, to acquire knowledge of God and his attributes. But Paley was not alone in Britain in the first half of the nineteenth century. A few years after the publication of *Natural Theology*, the eighth Earl of Bridgewater endowed the publication of treatises that would set forth "the Power, Wisdom and Goodness of God as manifested in the Creation." Eight treatises were published from 1833 to 1840, several of which artfully incorporate the best science of the time and had considerable influence among scientists and others. William Buckland, professor of geology at Oxford University, noted in *Geology and Mineralogy* (1836) the world distribution of coal and mineral ores and proceeded to point out that they had been deposited in a remote part, yet obviously with the forethought of serving the larger human populations that would come about much later. This attribution to the Creator is particularly noteworthy because in two earlier treatises, *Vindiciae Geologicae* (1820) and *Reliquiae Diluvianae* (1823), Buckland had explained sedimentation, fossil deposits, and rock formation as natural processes, without invoking the direct intervention of God.[12]

Another geologist, Hugh Miller, in *The Testimony of the Rocks* (1858) later developed what I will call the "argument-from-beauty." It is not only the perfection of design but also the beauty of natural structures found in rock formations and in mountains and rivers that manifests the intervention of the Creator.

One of the Bridgewater Treatises, *The Hand, Its Mechanisms and Vital Endowments as Evincing Design*, was written by Sir Charles Bell, a distinguished anatomist and surgeon, famous for his neurological discoveries, who became in 1836 professor of surgery at the University of Edinburgh. Bell follows Paley's manner of argument, examining in considerable detail the wondrously useful design of the human hand, but also the perfection of design of the forelimb used for different purposes in different animals, serving in each case the particular needs and habits of its owner. "It must now be apparent," he concluded, "that nothing less than the Power, which originally created, is equal to the effecting of those changes on animals, which are to adapt them to their conditions: that their organization is predetermined, and not consequent on the conditions of the earth or the surrounding elements."[13]

2

Charles Darwin

The Origin of Species

While he was an undergraduate student at the University of Cambridge between 1827 and 1831, Charles Darwin read Paley's *Natural Theology*, which was part of the university's curriculum for nearly half a century after Paley's death. Darwin writes in his *Autobiography* of the "much delight" and profit that he derived from reading Paley:

> In order to pass the B.A. examination, it was also necessary to get up Paley's *Evidences of Christianity*, and his *Moral Philosophy*. . . . The logic of . . . his *Natural Theology* gave me as much delight as did Euclid. . . . I did not at that time trouble myself about Paley's premises; and taking these on trust, I was charmed and convinced by the long line of argumentation.[1]

Charles Darwin (1809–1882) occupies an exalted place in the history of Western thought,

deservedly receiving credit for the theory of evolution. In *The Origin of Species*, published in 1859,
he accumulated evidence demonstrating the evolution of organisms. But accumulating evidence
for common descent with diversification may very
well have been a subsidiary objective of Darwin's
masterpiece. Darwin's *Origin of Species* is, first
and foremost, a sustained effort to solve Paley's
conundrum of how to account scientifically for
the design of organisms, but also for their imperfections, dysfunctions, oddities, and cruelties.

Darwin sought to explain the design of organisms—their complexity, diversity, and marvelous
contrivances—as the result of natural processes.
This is his primary theme. He discussed evolution as
well, since, as his work shows, biological evolution
is a necessary consequence of his theory of design
and thus corroborates this theory's cogency.

The argument developed in *Origin* may be separated into two components. The introduction and
chapters 1 through 8 of *Origin* explain how natural
selection accounts for the adaptations and behaviors of organisms—their design. In the concluding
chapter 14 of *The Origin of Species*, Darwin returns
to the dominant theme of adaptation and design.
The second component of Darwin's argument is the
evidence for evolution, which occupies chapters 9
to 13. If Darwin's explanation of the design of living beings is correct, evolution necessarily follows
as a consequence of organisms' becoming adapted
to different environments in different localities and
to the ever changing conditions of the environment

at different times. *Origin*'s evidence for biological evolution is central to Darwin's explanation of design, because his explanation implies that biological evolution occurs.

Origin's extended argument for natural selection starts in chapter 1, in which Darwin describes the successful selection of domestic plants and animals and, with considerable detail, the success of pigeon fanciers seeking exotic "sports." The success of plant and animal breeders manifests how much selection can accomplish by taking advantage of spontaneous variations that appear in organisms and happen to fit the breeders' objectives. The ensuing chapters extend the argument to variations propagated by natural selection for the benefit of the organisms themselves, rather than by artificial selection of traits desired by humans.

As a consequence of natural selection, organisms exhibit design, that is, adaptive organs and functions, but it is not "intelligent" design, imposed by God as a Supreme Engineer. Rather it is the result of a natural process of selection, promoting the adaptation of organisms to their environments. Individuals that have beneficial variations—ones that improve their probability of survival and reproduction—leave more descendants than do individuals of the same species that have less beneficial variations. The beneficial variations will consequently increase in frequency over the generations and extend to the whole species; less beneficial or harmful variations will eventually be eliminated from the species.

Organisms exhibit complex design, but it is not "irreducible" complexity, emerged all of a sudden in its current elaboration. Rather, according to Darwin's theory of natural selection, the design has arisen gradually and cumulatively, step by step, promoted by the reproductive success of individuals with incrementally more complex elaborations.

In the last paragraph of the final chapter (chapter 14) of *The Origin of Species*, Darwin asserts the "grandeur" of his vision:

> It is interesting to contemplate an entangled bank, clothed with many plants of many kinds, with birds singing on the bushes, with various insects flitting about, and with worms crawling through the damp earth, and to reflect that these *elaborately constructed* forms, *so different* from each other, and dependent on each other *in so complex a manner*, have all been produced by laws acting around us . . . Thus, from the war of nature, from famine and death, the most exalted object which we are capable of conceiving, namely, the production of the higher animals, directly follows.[2]

Darwin brings the book to an end, with this eloquent statement:

> There is grandeur in this view of life, with its several powers, having been originally breathed into a few forms or into one; and that, whilst this planet has gone cycling on

according to the fixed law of gravity, from so simple a beginning *endless forms most beautiful and most wonderful* have been, and are being, evolved."[3]

Darwin's *Origin* addresses the same issue as Paley: how to account for the adaptive configuration of organisms and their parts, which are so obviously "designed" to fulfill certain functions. Darwin argues that adaptive variations ("variations useful in some way to each being") occasionally appear, and that these are likely to increase the reproductive chances of their carriers. The success of pigeon fanciers and animal breeders clearly evinces the occasional occurrence of useful hereditary variations. In nature, over the generations, Darwin's argument continues, favorable variations will be preserved, multiplied, and conjoined; injurious ones will be eliminated. In one place, Darwin avers: "I can see no limit to this power [natural selection] in slowly and beautifully *adapting* each form to the most complex relations of life."[4]

Natural selection was proposed by Darwin primarily to account for the adaptive organization, or design, of living beings; it is a process that preserves and promotes adaptation. Evolutionary change through time and evolutionary diversification (multiplication of species) are not directly promoted by natural selection, but they often ensue as by-products of natural selection fostering adaptation.

The Copernican Revolution

Charles Darwin was the son and grandson of physicians. He enrolled as a medical student at the University of Edinburgh. After two years, however, he left and moved to the University of Cambridge to prepare to become a clergyman. He was not an exceptional student, but he was deeply interested in natural history. On December 27, 1831, a few months after his graduation from Cambridge, he sailed as a naturalist aboard the HMS *Beagle* on a 'round-the-world trip that lasted until October 1836. Darwin was often able to disembark for extended trips ashore to collect natural specimens.

The discovery of fossil bones from large extinct mammals in Argentina and the observation of numerous species of finches in the Galapagos Islands are among the events credited with stimulating Darwin's interest in how species originate. In addition to *The Origin of Species,* Darwin published many other books, notably *The Descent of Man and Selection in Relation to Sex* (1871), which extends the theory of natural selection to human evolution.

Darwin's revolution has been compared to the Copernican revolution that was launched three centuries earlier with the publication in 1543, the year of Nicolaus Copernicus's death, of his *De revolutionibus orbium celestium* ("On the Revolutions of the Celestial Spheres"), and bloomed with the publication in 1687 of Isaac Newton's *Philosophiae naturalis principia mathematica* ("The Mathematical Principles of Natural Philosophy").

According to a version of intellectual history, the Copernican revolution consisted in displacing the earth from its previously accepted locus as the center of the universe, moving it to a subordinate place as one more planet revolving around the sun. In congruous manner, the Darwinian revolution is viewed as consisting of the displacement of humans from their exalted position as the center of life on earth, with all other species created for the service of humankind. Copernicus had accomplished his revolution with the heliocentric theory of the solar system. Darwin's achievement emerged from his theory of organic evolution.

This version of the two revolutions is inadequate: what it says is true, but it misses what is most important about these two intellectual revolutions, namely, that they ushered in the beginning of science in the modern sense of the word. These two revolutions may jointly be seen as the one scientific revolution, with two stages, the Copernican and the Darwinian.

The discoveries of Copernicus, Kepler, Galileo, Newton, and others in the sixteenth and seventeenth centuries had gradually ushered in a conception of the universe as matter in motion governed by natural laws. It was shown that the earth is not the center of the universe but a small planet rotating around an average star; that the universe is immense in space and in time; and that the motions of the planets around the sun can be explained by the same simple laws that account for the motion of physical objects on our planet.

These laws include *force = mass* x *acceleration* and the so-called inverse square law of attraction between bodies such as the planets.

These and other discoveries greatly expanded human knowledge, but the conceptual revolution they brought about was more fundamental yet: a commitment to the postulate that the universe obeys immanent laws that account for natural phenomena. The workings of the universe were brought into the realm of science: explanation through natural laws. Physical phenomena could be accounted for whenever the causes were adequately known.

The advances of physical science brought about by the Copernican revolution had driven humankind's conception of the universe to a split-personality state of affairs, which persisted well into the mid-nineteenth century. By that time, scientific explanations derived from natural laws accounted for the world of nonliving matter, on the earth as well as in the heavens. Supernatural explanations, such as Paley's explanation of design, depending on the unfathomable deeds of the Creator, accounted for the origin and configuration of living creatures—the most diversified, complex, and interesting realities of the world.

Darwin's Revolution

It was Darwin's genius to resolve this conceptual bifurcation. Darwin completed the Copernican revolution by drawing out for biology the notion of nature as a lawful system of matter in motion that human reason can explain without recourse to extra-natural agencies.

The conundrum faced by Darwin can hardly be overestimated. The strength of the argument from design to demonstrate the role of the Creator had been forcefully set forth by Paley. Wherever there is function or design, we look for its author. It was Darwin's greatest accomplishment to show that the complex organization and functionality of living beings can be explained as the result of a natural process, natural selection, without any need to resort to a Creator or other external agent. The origin and adaptation of organisms in their profusion and wondrous variations were thus brought into the realm of science.

Darwin accepted that organisms are designed for certain purposes; that is, they are functionally organized. Organisms are adapted to certain ways of life, and their parts are adapted to perform certain functions. Fish are adapted to live in water; kidneys are designed to regulate the composition of blood; the human hand is made for grasping. But Darwin went on to provide a natural explanation of design. The seemingly purposeful aspects of living beings could now be explained, like the phenomena of the inanimate world, by the methods of science, as the result of natural laws manifested in natural processes.

That Darwin considered the discovery of natural selection (rather than his demonstration of evolution) his most important discovery emerges from consideration of his life and works. Recent historical studies have reinforced this conclusion:

Darwin designated natural selection, not evolution, as "my theory." The discovery of natural selection, Darwin's awareness that it is a greatly significant discovery as science's answer to Paley's argument from design, and its designation as "my theory" can be traced in Darwin's "Red" and "Transmutation Notebooks B to E," started in March 1837, not long after he returned on October 2, 1836, from his five-year trip on the HMS *Beagle*. These notebooks were completed in late 1839.[5]

The evolution of organisms was commonly accepted by naturalists in the middle decades of the nineteenth century. The distribution of exotic species in South America, the Galapagos Islands, and elsewhere, along with the discovery of fossil remains of long-extinguished animals, confirmed the reality of evolution in Darwin's mind. The intellectual challenge was to discover the explanation that would account for how new organisms adapted to their environments.

Early in the notebooks of 1837 and 1839, Darwin registers his discovery of natural selection ("my theory"). From then on, up until his death in 1882, Darwin's life would be dedicated to substantiating natural selection and its companion postulates, mainly the pervasiveness of hereditary variation and the enormous fertility of organisms, much surpassing the capacity of available resources. Natural selection became for Darwin "a theory by which to work." He relentlessly pursued observations and performed experiments in order to test the theory and resolve presumptive objections.

A Distinction with a Difference

On June 18, 1858, Darwin wrote to Charles Lyell that he had received by mail a short essay from Alfred Russell Wallace sketching natural selection as an explanation for evolutionary diversification. The essay was such that "if Wallace had my [manuscript] sketch written in [1844] he could not have made a better abstract."

At an emergency meeting of the Linnean Society of London on July 1, 1858, attended by some thirty people, three papers were read by the society's undersecretary, George Busk, in the order of their date of composition: Darwin's abbreviated abstract of his 230-page essay from 1844; an "abstract of abstract" that Darwin had written to the American botanist Asa Gray on September 5, 1857; and Wallace's essay, "On the Tendency of Varieties to Depart Indefinitely from Original Type; Instability of Varieties Supposed to Prove the Permanent Distinctness of Species."[6] The papers generated little response and virtually no discussion, their significance apparently unknown to those in attendance. Darwin and Wallace, who was at the time in the Malay archipelago, had started occasional correspondence in late 1855, with Darwin offering sympathy and encouragement to the occasionally dispirited Wallace for his "laborious undertaking" collecting valuable biological specimens.

Wallace (1823–1913) has been given credit for discovering, independently from Darwin, natural selection as the process accounting for the evolution of species. Wallace's independent discovery of natural selection is remarkable. Wallace's interest and motivation were not the explanation of design, however, but how to account for the evolution of species, as indicated in his paper's title. Wallace thought that evolution proceeds indefinitely and is progressive: "We believe that there is a tendency in nature to the continued progression of certain classes of varieties further and further from the original type—a progression to which there appears no reason to assign any definite limits."[7]

Darwin, on the contrary, did not accept that evolution would necessarily represent progress or advancement. Nor did he believe that evolution would always result in morphological change over time; rather, he knew of the existence of "living fossils," organisms that had remained unchanged for millions of years. For example, "some of the most ancient Silurian animals, as the Nautilus, Lingula, etc., do not differ much from living species."[8]

In 1858, Darwin was at work on a multivolume treatise, intended to be titled *On Natural Selection.* Wallace's paper stimulated Darwin to write *The Origin of Species,* which would be published the following year and which Darwin saw as an abbreviated essay of the much longer book he had intended to write. As noted earlier, Darwin's focus, in *The Origin* as elsewhere, was the explanation of design, with evolution playing the subsidiary role of supporting evidence.

After Darwin

Publication of *The Origin of Species* caused considerable public excitement. Scientists, politicians, clergymen, and notables of all kinds read and discussed the book, defending or deriding Darwin's ideas. The most visible actor in the controversies immediately following publication was the English biologist T. H. Huxley, known as "Darwin's bulldog," who defended the theory of evolution with articulate and sometimes mordant words, on public occasions as well as in numerous writings.

A younger English contemporary of Darwin, with considerable influence during the latter part of the nineteenth and in the early twentieth century, was Herbert Spencer. A philosopher rather than a biologist, he became an energetic proponent of evolutionary ideas, popularized a number of slogans, such as "survival of the fittest" (which was taken up by Darwin in later editions of the *Origin*), and engaged in social and metaphysical speculations.

Darwin's theory of evolution was intensely debated in the latter part of the nineteenth century and beyond. In the first three decades of the twentieth century, the controversy centered on the importance of genetic mutations relative to natural selection. Theoretical advances and the accumulation of experimental evidence resulted by the middle of the twentieth century in the formulation of the modern theory of evolution, which is generally accepted by biologists. Knowledge of evolutionary processes has continued to advance—and at an accelerated rate—into the present, often promoted by discoveries in other disciplines, such as molecular biology, paleontology, ecology, and genetics.

3

Evolution

Evolutionary Theories

Traditional Islam, Judaism, and Christianity explain the origin of living beings and their adaptations to their environments—wings, gills, hands, flowers—as the handiwork of an omniscient God. Among the early church fathers, Gregory of Nyssa (335–394) and Augustine maintained that not all of creation—not all species of plants and animals—were initially created by God; rather, some had evolved in historical times from God's creations. According to Gregory of Nyssa, the cosmic world has come about in two successive stages. The first stage, the creative step, is instantaneous; the second stage, the formative step, is gradual and develops through time. According to Augustine, many plant and animal species were not directly created by God, but only indirectly, in their potentiality (in their *rationes seminales*), so that they would come about by natural processes, later in the history of the world.

The notion that organisms may change by natural processes was not scientifically investigated by Christian theologians of the Middle Ages, but it was, usually incidentally, considered as a possibility by many, including Albertus Magnus (1200–1280) and his student Thomas Aquinas. Thomas concluded, after detailed discussion, that the development of living creatures, such as maggots and flies, from nonliving matter, such as decaying meat, was not incompatible with Christian faith or philosophy. But he left it to others (to scientists, in current parlance) to determine whether this actually happened.

The issue of whether living organisms could spontaneously arise from dead matter was not settled until four centuries later by the Italian Francesco Redi (1626–1697), one of the first scientists to conduct biological experiments with proper controls. Redi set up flasks with various kinds of fresh meat, some were sealed, others covered with gauze so that air but not flies could enter, and others left uncovered. Maggots appeared only in the uncovered flasks, which flies had entered freely.

The cause of putrefaction was discovered two centuries later by the Frenchman Louis Pasteur (1822–1895). Pasteur demonstrated that fermentation and putrefaction were caused by minute organisms that could be destroyed by heat. Food decomposes when placed in contact with germs present in the air; germs do not spontaneously generate within the food.

A theory of evolution was proposed by the French naturalist Jean-Baptiste de Monet, chevalier de Lamarck (1744–1829). In his *Philosophie zoologique* ("Zoological Philosophy," 1809), Lamarck held that living organisms represent a progression, with humans as the highest form. Organisms evolve through eons of time from lower to higher forms, a process still going on, always culminating in human beings. The remote ancestors of humans were worms and other inferior creatures, which gradually evolved into more and more advanced organisms. Lamarck's evolution theory was more metaphysical than scientific. Lamarck postulated that life possesses an innate property to improve over time, so that progression from lower to higher organisms would continually occur, so that today's worms will yield humans as their remote descendants. As animals become adapted to their environments through their habits, modifications occur. Use of an organ or structure reinforces it; disuse leads to obliteration. The characteristics acquired by use and disuse, according to this theory, would be inherited.[1]

Erasmus Darwin (1731–1802), a physician and poet and the grandfather of Charles Darwin, proposed, in poetic rather than scientific language, a theory of the transmutation of life forms through eons of time (*Zoonomia, or the Laws of Organic Life*, 1794–1796).

Darwin and the Voyage of the *Beagle*

The observations Darwin made in the Galapagos Islands as part of his trip on the *Beagle* may have been the most influential on his thinking. The islands, on the equator six hundred miles off the west coast of South America, had been named *Galápagos* (the Spanish word for tortoises) because of the abundance of giant tortoises, which varied among the different islands and differed from those known anywhere else in the world. The tortoises sluggishly clanked their way around, feeding on the vegetation and seeking the few pools of fresh water. They would have been vulnerable to predators, which were conspicuously absent on the islands. In the Galapagos, Darwin found large lizards feeding on seaweed that were unlike any others of their kind and mockingbirds quite different from those found on the South American mainland. His most well-known discovery was several kinds of finches, which varied from island to island, with distinctive beaks adapted to disparate feeding habits: crushing nuts, probing for insects, grasping worms.

Arguing for Evolution

Darwin and other nineteenth-century biologists found compelling evidence for biological evolution in the comparative study of living organisms, in their geographic distribution, and in the fossil remains of extinct organisms. Since Darwin's time, the evidence from these sources has become stronger and more comprehensive, while biological disciplines that have emerged recently—genetics, biochemistry, physiology, ecology, animal behavior (ethology), and especially molecular biology—have supplied powerful additional evidence and detailed confirmation.

Evolutionists no longer are concerned with obtaining evidence to support the fact of evolution but rather are concerned with what sorts of knowledge can be obtained from different biological disciplines. I will now briefly summarize several types of information used as evidence for evolution. Among the immensity of new evidence acquired since Darwin's time, I will particularly draw attention to the evolution of our hominid ancestors, which I will review in the next chapter.

The Fossil Record

Paleontologists have recovered and studied the fossil remains of many thousands of organisms that lived in the past. This fossil record shows that many kinds of extinct organisms were very different in form from any now living. The fossil record also shows successions of organisms through time, manifesting their transition from one form to another.

When an organism dies, its body is usually destroyed by other forms of life and by weathering processes. On rare occasions some body parts—particularly hard ones such as shells, teeth, and bones—are preserved by being buried in mud or protected in some other way from predators and weather, and they may be preserved indefinitely with the rocks in which they are embedded. Methods such as radiometric dating—measuring the amounts of natural radioactive atoms that remain in certain minerals—make it possible to estimate the time period when the rocks, and the fossils associated with them, were formed.

Radiometric dating indicates that the earth was formed about 4.5 billion years ago. The earliest fossils resemble microorganisms such as bacteria; the oldest of these fossils appear in rocks 3.5 billion years old. The oldest known animal fossils, about 700 million years old, come from the so-called *Ediacara* fauna, small wormlike creatures with soft bodies. Numerous fossils belonging to many living phyla[2] and exhibiting mineralized skeletons appear in rocks about 540 million years old. These organisms are different from organisms living now and from those living at intervening times. Some are so radically different that paleontologists have created new phyla in order to classify them. The first vertebrates, or animals with backbones, appeared about 400 million years ago; the first mammals, less than 200 million years ago. The history of life recorded by fossils presents compelling evidence of evolution.

The fossil record is incomplete. Of the small proportion of organisms preserved as fossils, only a tiny fraction has been recovered and studied by paleontologists. In some cases the succession of forms over time has been reconstructed with much detail. One example is the evolution of the horse, which can be traced to an animal the size of a dog having several toes on each foot and teeth appropriate for browsing; this animal, called the dawn horse (genus *Hyracotherium*), lived more than fifty million years ago. The most recent form, the modern horse (*Equus*), is much larger in size, is one-toed, and has teeth appropriate for grazing. Transitional forms are well preserved as fossils, as are other kinds of extinct horses that evolved in different directions and left no living descendants.

For skeptical contemporaries of Darwin, the "missing link"—the absence of any known transitional form between apes and humans—was a battle cry. Not one but many creatures intermediate between living apes and humans have since been found as fossils, as will be reviewed in the next chapter. Here I want to mention two other examples of "missing links" that are no longer missing: *Tiktaalik*, intermediate between fish and tetrapods, and *Archaeopteryx*, intermediate between reptiles and birds.

Paleontologists have known for more than a century that tetrapods (four-limbed animals: amphibians, reptiles, birds, and mammals) evolved from a particular group of fishes called "lobe-finned." Until recently, *Panderichthys* was the known fossil fish closest to the tetrapods. *Panderichthys* was somewhat crocodile shaped, with a pectoral fin skeleton and shoulder girdle that are intermediate in shape between those of typical lobe-finned fishes and those of tetrapods. *Panderichthys* is known from Latvia, where it lived around the mid-Devonian period, some 385 million years ago.

Until recently, the earliest fish-like tetrapod fossils were also from the Devonian, about 376 million years old, from Scotland and Latvia. Thus, the time gap between the most tetrapod-like fish and the most fish-like tetrapods was nearly ten million years, between 385 and 376 million years ago. The morphological gap was also substantial, because none of these animals was a true intermediate between fish and tetrapods.

A recently discovered fossil (published in April 2006), known as *Tiktaalik*, goes a long way toward bridging this gap. It is the most nearly intermediate between fishes and tetrapods yet known.[3] Several specimens have been found in late Devonian river sediments, dated about 380 million years ago, on Ellesmere Island in Nunavut, part of Arctic Canada. *Tiktaalik* is Inuit for "big freshwater fish." *Tiktaalik* was a flattened, superficially crocodile-like animal. Fish-like features include small pelvic fins, fin rays rather than digits in their paired appendages, and well-developed gill arches, which suggest that they remained mostly aquatic. But the bony gill cover has disappeared, indicating reduced water flow through the gill chamber. The elongated snout suggests a shift from sucking toward snapping up prey, mostly on land. The relatively large ribs indicate that *Tiktaalik* could support its body out of water.

The first *Archaeopteryx* was discovered in Bavaria in 1861, two years after the publication of Darwin's *Origin*, and received much attention because it shed light on the origin of birds and bolstered Darwin's postulate of the existence of missing links. Other *Archaeopteryx* specimens have been discovered in the last hundred years. The most recent—the tenth—was described in

December 2005. It is the best preserved *Archae-opteryx* yet.[4]

Archaeopteryx lived during the Late Jurassic period, about sixty million years ago, and exhibited a mixture of both avian and reptilian traits. All specimens known are small, about the size of a crow, and share many anatomical characteristics with some of the smaller bipedal dinosaurs. *Archaeopteryx's* skeleton is reptile-like, but it had feathers, clearly shown in the fossils, a bird-like skull with expanded braincase, large eye sockets, and a pronounced beak. Unlike modern birds, however, it had teeth. *Archaeopteryx* may have been capable of flying but not of sustained flight.

Morphological Similarities

Comparative anatomy investigates the homologies, or inherited similarities, among organisms in bone structure and in other parts of the body. The correspondence of structures is typically very close among some organisms—the different varieties of songbirds, for instance—but becomes less so as the organisms being compared are less closely related in their evolutionary history. The similarities are less between mammals and birds than they are among mammal species, and they are still less between mammals and fishes. Similarities in structure help to reconstruct the phylogeny, or evolutionary history, of organisms.

Comparative anatomy reveals why most organismic structures are not perfect. The skeletons of turtles, horses, humans, birds, whales, and bats are strikingly similar, in spite of these animals' different ways of life and the diversity of their environments. The correspondence, bone by bone, can easily be seen in the limbs as well as in other parts of the body. From a purely practical point of view, it seems incomprehensible that a turtle and a whale should swim, a horse run, a person write, and a bird or bat fly with forelimb structures built of the same bones. An engineer could design better limbs in each case. But if it is accepted that all of these animals inherited their skeleton structures from a common ancestor and became modified only as they adapted to different ways of life, the similarity of their structures makes sense.

An organism's body parts are less than perfectly adapted because they are modified from an inherited structure rather than designed from completely raw materials for a specific purpose. The anatomy of animals reflects that it has been designed to fit their lifestyles. But it is "imperfect" design, accomplished by natural selection, rather than "intelligent" design. The imperfection of structures is evidence for evolution and contrary to the arguments for intelligent design.

Embryonic Development and Vestiges

Vertebrates, from fishes through lizards to humans, develop in ways that are remarkably similar during early stages, but they become more and more differentiated as the embryos approach maturity. The similarities persist longer between organisms that are more closely related (for example, humans and monkeys) than between those less closely related (humans and sharks).

The embryos of humans and other nonaquatic vertebrates exhibit gill slits even though they never breathe through gills. These slits are found in the embryos of all vertebrates because they share a common ancestor: the fish in which these structures first evolved.

Human embryos also exhibit by the fourth week of development a well-defined tail, which reaches maximum length at six weeks. Similar embryonic tails are found in other mammals, such as dogs, horses, and monkeys; in humans, however, the tail eventually shortens, persisting only as a rudiment in the adult coccyx. Embryonic rudiments are inconsistent with claims of intelligent design.

Embryonic rudiments that never fully develop, such as the gill slits in humans, are common in all sorts of animals. Some, however, like the tail rudiment in humans, persist as adult vestiges, reflecting evolutionary ancestry. A familiar rudimentary organ in humans is the vermiform appendix. This wormlike structure attaches to a short section of intestine called the cecum, which is located at the point where the large and small intestines join. The human vermiform appendix is a functionless vestige of a fully developed organ present in other mammals, such as the rabbit and other herbivores, where a large cecum and appendix store vegetable cellulose to enable its digestion with the help of bacteria.

Vestiges are instances of imperfections—like the imperfections seen in anatomical structures—that argue against creation by design but are fully understandable as a result of evolution by natural selection.

The Geography of Life

There are about 1,500 known species of *drosophila* fruitflies in the world; nearly one-third of them live in Hawaii and nowhere else. Also in Hawaii are more than one thousand species of snails and other land mollusks that exist nowhere else. This unusual diversity is easily explained by evolution. The islands of Hawaii are extremely isolated and have had few colonizers—that is, animals and plants that arrived from elsewhere. Those species that did colonize the islands found many unoccupied ecological niches (local environments suited to sustaining them), which, moreover, lacked predators that would prevent them from multiplying. In response, these species rapidly diversified; this process of diversifying in order to fill ecological niches is called adaptive radiation.

Each of the world's continents has its own distinctive collection of animals and plants. In Africa are rhinoceroses, hippopotamuses, lions, hyenas, giraffes, zebras, lemurs, monkeys with narrow noses and nonprehensile tails, chimpanzees, and gorillas. South America, which extends over much the same latitudes as Africa, has none of these animals; instead, it has pumas, jaguars, tapirs, llamas, raccoons, opossums, armadillos, and monkeys with broad noses and large prehensile tails, but not apes.

These vagaries of biogeography are not due to the different suitability of different environments. There is no reason to believe that South American animals are not well suited to living in Africa or those of Africa to living in South America. The islands of Hawaii are no better suited than other Pacific islands for *drosophila* fruitflies, nor are they less hospitable than other parts of the world for many absent organisms. In fact, although no land mammals are native to the Hawaiian islands, pigs and goats have multiplied there as wild animals after they were introduced by humans. The absence of many species from a hospitable environment in which an extraordinary variety of other species flourish can be explained by the theory of evolution, which holds that species can exist and evolve only in geographic areas that were colonized by their ancestors.

Molecular Biology

Molecular biology provides the most detailed and convincing evidence available for biological evolution. A remarkable uniformity exists in the molecular components of organisms—in the nature of the components as well as in the ways in which they are assembled and used. In all bacteria, plants, animals, and humans, the DNA comprises sequences of the same four component nucleotides, and all the various proteins are synthesized from different combinations and sequences of the same twenty amino acids.[5]

Genes and proteins are long molecules that contain information in the sequence of their components in much the same way as sentences of the English language contain information in the sequence of their letters and words. The sequences that make up the genes are passed on from parents to offspring, identical except for occasional changes introduced by mutations. Closely related species have very similar DNA sequences; the few differences reflect mutations that occurred since their last common ancestor. Species that are less closely related to one another exhibit more differences in their DNA than those more closely related. The similarity between DNA sequences from different species is evidence that they have evolved from a common ancestor.

As an illustration, let us assume that we are comparing two books. Both books are two hundred pages long and contain the same number of chapters. Closer examination reveals that the two books are identical page for page and word for word, except that an occasional word—say, one in one hundred—is different. The two books cannot have been written independently; either one has been copied from the other, or both have been copied, directly or indirectly, from the same original book. In living beings, if each component nucleotide of DNA is represented by one letter, printing the complete sequence of nucleotides in the DNA of a higher organism would require hundreds of books, each with hundreds of pages, with several thousand letters on each page. When the pages (or sequences of nucleotides) in these books are examined one by one, the correspondence in the letters (nucleotides) gives unmistakable evidence of common origin.

The degree of similarity in the sequence of nucleotides or of amino acids can be precisely quantified. For example, in humans and chimpanzees, the protein molecule called cytochrome-c, which serves a vital function in respiration within cells, consists of the same 104 amino acids in exactly the same order. It differs, however, from the cytochrome-c of rhesus monkeys by one amino acid, from that of horses by eleven additional amino acids, and from that of tuna by twenty-one additional amino acids. The degree of similarity reflects the recency of common ancestry. Thus, the inferences from comparative anatomy and other disciplines concerning evolutionary history can be tested in molecular studies of DNA and proteins by examining their sequences of nucleotides and amino acids.

The authority of this kind of test is overwhelming; each of the thousands of genes and thousands of proteins contained in an organism provides an independent test of that organism's evolutionary history. Many thousands of tests have been done, and not one has given evidence contrary to evolution. Molecular biology, a discipline that emerged in the second half of the twentieth century, nearly one hundred years after the publication of *The Origin of Species*, has provided the strongest evidence yet of the evolution of organisms. There is probably no other notion in any field of science that has been as extensively tested and as thoroughly corroborated as the evolutionary origin of living organisms.

The Universal Tree of Life

Molecular biology has made possible the reconstruction of the universal tree of life, which embraces all living organisms from LUCA (the Last Universal Common Ancestor), which lived more than three billion years ago, to the present. Groups of organisms are represented by the branches of the tree. There are three major sets of branches: bacteria, archaea, and eukarya. Eukaryotes are all organisms with complex cells, which contain several organelles, one of which, the nucleus, includes the DNA that embodies the genetic information. Bacteria and archaea are prokaryotes; the DNA in their cells is not enclosed in a nucleus ("prokaryote" means "without nucleus"). They are microscopic organisms. Most eukaryotic organisms are also microscopic single cells. Animals, plants, and fungi are multicellular organisms—the only ones that can be directly perceived by our senses—but they are only three of the many branches of the eukaryotes. All organisms, prokaryotes and eukaryotes, are related by common descent from LUCA.

It is now possible to assert that gaps of knowledge in the evolutionary history of living organisms no longer exist. This statement will come as a surprise to those who have heard again and again about "missing links," about the absence of fossil intermediates between reptiles and birds or between fish and tetrapods, and about the "Cambrian explosion." The evolutionary explosion that has occurred in recent years concerns knowledge, not the Cambrian: molecular biology has made it possible to reconstruct the universal tree of life, the continuity of succession from the original forms of life (ancestral to all living organisms) to every species now living on earth. The main branches of the tree of life have been reconstructed on the whole and in many details. More details about more and more branches of the universal tree of life are published in scores of scientific articles every month. The virtually unlimited evolutionary information encoded in the DNA sequence of living organisms allows evolutionists to reconstruct all evolutionary relationships leading to present-day organisms, with as much detail as desired. Invest the necessary resources (time and laboratory expenses), and you can have the answer to any query, with as much precision as you may want.

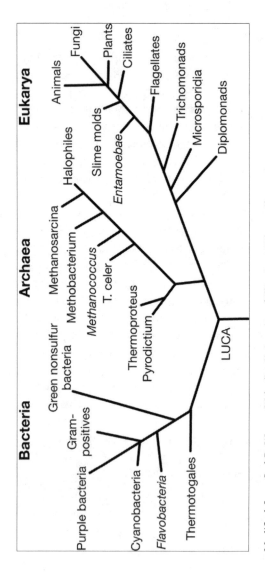

Modified from Carl R. Woese, Web site, University of Illinois at Urbana-Champaign, Department of Microbiology

4

Human Evolution

A common challenge to Darwin's theory was the "missing link" between humans and apes. No fossils were known in Darwin's time that would have likely been our ancestors after the human lineage separated from the apes, our closest relatives. The missing link is no longer missing. Hundreds of fossil remains belonging to hundreds of intermediate human ancestors have been discovered since Darwin's time and continue to be discovered at an accelerated rate. The fossils that belong to the human lineage after its separation from the ape lineages are called hominids.

The oldest known fossil hominids are six million to seven million years old, come from Africa, and are known as *Sahelanthropus* and *Orrorin* (or *Praeanthropus*). These ancestors were predominantly bipedal when on the ground but had very small brains. *Ardipithecus* lived about 4.4 million years ago, also in Africa. Numerous fossil remains from diverse African origins are known as *Australopithecus*, a hominid that appeared between three million and four million years ago. *Australopithecus* had an upright human stance but a cranial capacity of less than five hundred cubic centimeters (equivalent to a brain weight of about five hundred grams, a bit more than one pound), comparable to that of a gorilla or chimpanzee and about one-third that of modern humans. Its head displayed a mixture of ape and human characteristics—a low forehead and a long, apelike face but with teeth proportioned like those of humans. Other early hominids partly contemporaneous with *Australopithecus* include *Kenyanthropus* and *Paranthropus*; both had comparatively small brains, although some species of *Paranthropus* had larger bodies. *Paranthropus* represents a side branch of the hominid lineage that became extinct.

Along with increased cranial capacity, other human characteristics have been found in *Homo habilis*, which lived about 1.5 million to 2 million years ago in Africa and had a cranial capacity of more than six hundred cubic centimeters (about one and one-third pounds), and in *Homo erectus*, which evolved in Africa somewhat before 1.8 million years ago and had a cranial capacity of eight hundred to 1,100 cubic centimeters (from nearly two pounds to nearly two and a half pounds).

Homo erectus is the first intercontinental migrant among our hominid ancestors. Shortly after its emergence in Africa, *Homo erectus* spread to Europe and Asia, even as far as the Indonesian archipelago and northern China. Fossil remains of *Homo erectus* have been found in Africa, Indonesia

(Java), China, the Middle East, and Europe. *Homo erectus* fossils from Java have been dated at 1.81 and 1.66 million years ago, and from Georgia (in Europe, near the Asian border) between 1.6 and 1.8 million years ago. Several species of hominids lived in Africa, Europe, and Asia between 1.8 million and 500,000 years ago; they are known as *Homo ergaster*, *Homo antecessor*, and *Homo heidelbergensis*, with brain sizes roughly that of the brain of *Homo erectus*. Some of these species were partly contemporaneous, though they lived in different regions of the Old World.

The transition from *Homo erectus* to *Homo sapiens* occurred around 400,000 years ago. *Homo erectus* persisted in Asia until 250,000 years ago in China and perhaps until 100,000 years ago in Java. The species *Homo neanderthalensis* appeared in Europe more than 200,000 years ago and persisted until 30,000 years ago. The Neanderthals had been thought to be ancestral to anatomically modern humans, but now we know that modern humans appeared at least 100,000 years ago, long before the disappearance of Neanderthal fossils. It is puzzling that, in caves in the Middle East, fossils of anatomically modern humans precede as well as follow Neanderthal fossils. Some modern humans from these caves are dated at 120,000 to 100,000 years ago, whereas Neanderthals are dated at 60,000 and 70,000 years, followed by modern humans dated at 40,000 years. It is unclear whether the two forms repeatedly replaced one another by migration from other regions, or whether they coexisted, or indeed whether interbreeding may have occurred (although comparisons of DNA from Neanderthal fossils with living humans indicate that no, or very little, interbreeding occurred between Neanderthals and their contemporary anatomically modern humans.)

Lucy

Lucy is the whimsical name given to the fossil remains of a hominid ancestor classified as *Australopithecus afarensis*, a species of bipedal hominids, small brained and some three and a half feet tall. Lucy is duly famous because about 40 percent of the whole skeleton of this adolescent girl was found on a single site when it was discovered thirty years ago. Experts generally agree that *Australopithecus afarensis*, who lived between 3 million and 3.6 million years ago, is in the line of descent to modern humans.

Australopithecus africanus, who lived more recently and is the first *Australopithecus* species ever discovered, also short and small-brained, is rather a co-lateral relative, the likely ancestor of *Paranthropus robustus* and other co-lateral hominids, who lived for two million years or more after their divergence from our ancestral lineage and thus long coexisted in Africa with some of our ancestors. Some of these co-lateral relatives became somewhat taller and more robust, but their brains remained small—about five hundred to six hundred cubic centimeters at the most.

The discovery of hominid fossils has increased at an accelerated rate over the last two decades.

In 1994, *Ardipithecus ramidus* from Ethiopia was discovered, a more primitive hominid than *Australopithecus*, soon followed by *Australopithecus anamensis* from Kenya (dated about 3.9 to about 4.2 million years ago), as well as more specimens of *Ardipithecus* (some as old as about 5.5 to 5.8 million years) and the already mentioned *Sahelanthropus* (around six to seven million years old from Chad) and *Orrorin* (about 5.7 to six million years old from Kenya). The position of these fossil hominids, whether in the direct ancestry of *Homo* or as co-lateral relatives remains a subject of debate. It has been commonly assumed, however, that *Australopithecus anamensis*, dated around 3.9 to 4.2 million years ago, is the ancestral species to *Australopithecus afarensis*, whose earliest definitive specimen is about 3.6 million years old.

The analysis and publication, on April 13, 2006, of thirty additional hominid specimens, representing a minimum of eight individuals, of *Australopithecus anamensis* from the Afar region of Ethiopia, dated to about 4.12 million years ago supports the interpretation that *Australopithecus anamensis* is ancestral to *Australopithecus afarensis* and in the direct line of descent to modern humans.[1] The new fossils suggest, moreover, that *Ardipithecus* was the ancestor of *Australopithecus anamensis* and all later australopithecines. These fossils suggest that a relatively rapid evolution from *Ardipithecus* to *Australopithecus* occurred in the Afar region of Ethiopia.

Origin of Modern Humans

Some anthropologists argue that the transition from *Homo erectus* to archaic *Homo sapiens*, and later to anatomically modern humans, occurred consonantly in various parts of the Old World, Africa, Asia, and perhaps Europe. Most scientists argue instead that modern humans first arose in Africa somewhat earlier than 100,000 years ago and spread from there throughout the world, replacing the preexisting populations of *Homo erectus* and related hominid species, including *Homo neanderthalensis*. Some proponents of this African replacement model argue further that the transition from archaic to modern *Homo sapiens* was associated with a very narrow bottleneck, perhaps of only a few thousand individuals, who are the ancestors of all modern humans.

Recent analyses of DNA from living humans have confirmed the African origin of modern *Homo sapiens*, which is dated by these analyses at about 156,000 years ago in tropical Africa. Shortly thereafter modern humans spread through Africa and from Africa throughout the world. Southeast Asia and the region that is now China were colonized by sixty thousand years ago. Shortly thereafter, modern humans reached Australasia, New Guinea, and Australia. Europe was colonized more recently, only about thirty-five thousand years ago, and America even more recently, perhaps only fifteen thousand years ago. Ethnic differentiation among modern human populations is therefore evolutionarily recent, a result of divergent evolution in geographically separated populations during less than 100,000 years.

Brain and Mind

Two conspicuous features of human anatomy are erect posture and large brain. Generally, in mammals, brain size is proportional to body size; relative to body mass, humans have the largest (and most complex) brain among all mammals. The chimpanzee's brain weighs less than a pound; a gorilla's slightly more. Our hominid ancestors had, since at least five million years ago, a bipedal gait, but their brain was small, little more than a pound in weight, until about two million years ago. Brain size increased notably starting with our *Homo habilis* ancestors, who had a brain of about one and one-third pounds. Our *Homo habilis* ancestors are the first known tool makers (hence the name *habilis*, Latin for "of things"). This species persisted for a few hundred thousand years (from about 1.5 million to 2 million years ago; see discussion earlier in this chapter). Their descendants, *Homo erectus*, had adult brains reaching up to somewhat more than two pounds in weight. Our species, *Homo sapiens*, has a brain of about three pounds, three times as large as that of the early hominids.

The draft DNA sequence of the chimpanzee genome was published on September 1, 2005. In the genome regions shared by humans and chimpanzees, the two species are 99 percent identical.

The differences appear to be very small or quite large, depending on how one chooses to look at them: 1 percent of the total seems very little, but it amounts to a difference of thirty million DNA letters out of the three billion in each genome. Some 29 percent of the enzymes and other proteins encoded by the genes are identical in both species. Out of the one hundred to several hundred amino acids that make up each protein, the 71 percent of nonidentical proteins differ between humans and chimps by only two amino acids, on average. The two genomes are about 96 percent identical if one takes into account DNA stretches found in one species but not the other. That is, a large amount of genetic material, about 3 percent or some ninety million DNA letters, has been inserted or deleted in one or the other species, since the time when humans and chimps initiated their separate evolutionary ways, seven or eight million years ago. Most of this inserted or deleted DNA does not contain genes coding for proteins.

Our brain is not only much larger than that of chimpanzees or gorillas, but also much more complex. The cerebral cortex, where the higher cognitive functions are processed, is in humans disproportionally much greater than the rest of the brain, when compared to apes.

The human brain consists of thirty billion nerve cells, or neurons, each connected to many others through two kinds of cell extensions, known as the axon and the dendrites (there are nearly one quadrillion connections between all neurons of the brain). From the evolutionary point of view, the animal brain is a powerful biological adaptation; it allows an organism to obtain and process information about environmental conditions and then to react adaptively to them. This ability has been carried to the limit in humans, in which the extravagant hypertrophy of the brain makes possible abstract thinking, language, and technology.

5

Natural Selection

Natural selection may be defined, most simply, as the differential reproduction of hereditary variations. Behind this simple definition there is an enormous amount of knowledge: mathematical, conceptual, and experimental. The definition I have given is comparable to defining the molecular theory of matter by saying that all matter is composed of molecules, or defining plate tectonics as the motion of the continental plates around the earth. Similarly as in these cases, or even more so, there are many books and innumerable scientific papers in which the complexities and variations of the process of natural selection are investigated, appropriate mathematical models and equations are developed that account for the process of natural selection, and the results of laboratory experiments and investigations of natural selection in nature are reported. As we saw in chapter 3, Darwin dedicated much of *The Origin* to the demonstration and explanation of natural selection. Moreover, Darwin wrote several other books further expanding how natural selection works—books dedicated, for example, to the evolution of orchids, barnacles, earthworms, primates, and humans.

I cannot here review or even summarize this extensive knowledge. What I can do is describe some elements of the process, seeking to explain how natural selection accounts for the design of organisms.

Adaptation, Design, Evolution

Scientists typically use the term *adaptation* rather than *design* when they speak about organisms and their features. For example, scientists speak of the gills as adaptations for breathing in water and lungs as adaptations for breathing in air; of legs as adaptations for walking or running and wings as adaptations for flying; of nesting as an adaptation for breeding helpless chicks and breast feeding as an adaptation to nourish immature calves or babies. Scientists could also say that gills are "designed" for breathing in water, lungs are "designed" for breathing in air, and similarly for the other examples. But the common use of *design* in the English language refers to the creations of artists and engineers and, thus, to the actions of designing agents, external to the designed objects. The intended meaning of the proponents of intelligent design is precisely this; namely, that organisms and their features have been designed by an external agent, God. But the adaptations of organisms, their designed features, are outcomes of natural selection, rather than constructions of a designing agent. Scientists speak of *adaptation* rather than *design* so as to exclude the connotation of a designing agent.

One important point to add is that natural selection primarily promotes adaptation rather than evolution. Individuals that happen to have variations that are adaptive (that is, that are beneficial to them) in the environment where the organisms live will likely leave more progeny than individuals with less beneficial variations, because the former survive better or because they are more fertile. For example, a swifter gazelle will be more successful at evading predators, and a hen with larger ovaries may produce more chicks. Thus, in the next generation, the beneficial variations will be more numerously represented than the alternative, less beneficial variations. The beneficial variations will be shared, after some or many generations, by all individuals in the species; harmful or less beneficial variations will have been eliminated.

As natural selection of adaptive variations takes place, evolutionary change occurs. Over the generations, some variations completely replace others, which when it happens again and again over thousands and millions of generations will result in substantial change: evolution that can be detected in the fossil record or otherwise. The rate of evolution will be greater when the environment changes faster and when organisms move from one habitat to another, say from a warmer to a colder climate or from a forest to a grassland.

Darwin's Natural Selection

This is how Darwin summarizes the process of natural selection:

> Can it, then, be thought improbable, seeing that variations useful to man have undoubtedly occurred, that other variations useful in some way to each being in the great and complex battle of life, should sometimes occur in the course of thousands of generations? If such do occur, can we doubt (remembering that more individuals are born than can possibly survive) that individuals having any advantage, however slight, over others, would have the best chance of surviving and of procreating their kind? On the other hand, we may feel sure that any variation in the least degree injurious would be rigidly destroyed. This preservation of favorable variations and the rejection of injurious variations, I call Natural Selection.[1]

Darwin addresses the same issues as Paley did: how to account for the adaptive configuration of organisms, the obvious design of their parts to fulfill certain functions. Darwin's argument starts with the existence of adaptive variations ("variations useful in some way to each being"). Experience with animal husbandry and plant breeding had demonstrated to Darwin that variations occur that are "useful" to humankind. So, he reasoned, variations must occur in nature that are favorable or useful in some way to the organisms themselves in the struggle for existence. Favorable variations are those that increase chances for survival and procreation. The advantageous variations are preserved and multiplied from generation to generation at the expense of less advantageous ones. This is the process of natural selection. The outcomes of the process are organisms that are well adapted to their habitats; evolution occurs as a consequence.

Natural selection, then, can be defined as the "differential reproduction of alternative hereditary variations," as I did at the beginning of this chapter, but I could add: "determined by the fact that some variations increase the likelihood that the organisms having them will survive and reproduce more successfully than will organisms carrying alternative variations." I could add still more and more details; whole books have been written about natural selection. The essence of the process, as I have stated it, is that over the generations, favorable variations will be preserved, multiplied, and conjoined; injurious ones will be eliminated. Evolutionary change through time and evolutionary diversification ensue as by-products of natural selection fostering adaptation.

Evolution as Genetic Change

Biological evolution is the process of change and diversification of living things over time, and it affects all aspects of their lives—morphology (form and structure), physiology, behavior, and ecology. Underlying these changes are changes in the hereditary materials. Hence, in genetic terms, evolution consists of changes in the organisms' hereditary makeup.

Evolution can be seen as a two-step process. First, hereditary variation arises; second, selection occurs of those genetic variations that are passed on most effectively to the following generations. That is, the variations that arise by spontaneous mutation are not transmitted equally from one generation to another. Some may become more frequent because they are favorable to the organisms in which they occur.

Hereditary variations, favorable or not to the organisms, arise by a process known as "mutation." Mutation is a random process with respect to adaptation. Mutations arise without regard for the consequences they may have in the ability of the organisms to survive and reproduce. If mutation were the only process of evolutionary change, the organization of living things would gradually disintegrate. The effects of mutation alone would be analogous to those of a mechanic who changed parts in an automobile engine at random, with no regard for the role of the parts in the engine. Natural selection keeps the disorganizing effects of mutation and other processes in check because it multiplies beneficial mutations and eliminates harmful ones.

Natural selection accounts not only for the preservation and improvement of the organization of living beings but also for their diversity. In different localities or in different circumstances, natural selection favors different traits, precisely those that make the organisms well adapted to their particular habitats and ways of life.

Mutations and DNA

Life originated about 3.5 billion years ago. The primordial organisms were very small and relatively simple. All living things have evolved from these lowly beginnings. At present there are more than two million known species, which are widely diverse in size, shape, and way of life. These differences are grounded on molecules of DNA, a double-helix molecule that carries information in the long sequence of its four components, represented by the letters A, C, G, and T. The genetic information of an organism is contained in sequences of these letters, in a manner analogous to the way semantic information is conveyed by sequences of letters of the alphabet. The amount of genetic information in organisms is enormous, because the total length of the DNA molecules of an organism is huge. For example, the human genome, which is the DNA that each human inherits from each parent, is three billion letters long. Printing one human genome would require one thousand books, each containing one thousand pages, with three thousand letters (about five hundred words) per page. Scientists do not print full genomes of humans or other organisms; rather, the DNA information is stored electronically in computers.

The information encoded in the nucleotide sequence of DNA is, as a rule, faithfully reproduced during replication, so that each replication results in two DNA molecules that are identical to each other and to the parent molecule. But heredity is not a perfectly conservative process. Occasionally "mistakes," or mutations, occur in the DNA molecule during replication, so that daughter cells differ from the parent cells in the sequence or in the amount of DNA, usually by only one letter but sometimes by many letters. A mutation first appears in a single cell of an organism, but it is passed on to all cells descended from the first.

Mutation rates have been measured in a great variety of organisms, mostly for mutants that exhibit conspicuous effects. In humans and other multicellular organisms, the rate typically ranges from about 1 per 100,000 to 1 per 1,000,000 sex cells. Although mutation rates are low, new mutants appear continuously in nature, because there are many individuals in every species and lots of DNA in every individual. The human population consists of more than six billion people. If any given possible mutation occurs once in each million people, living humans will collectively carry six thousand copies of every possible mutation.

The process of mutation provides each generation with many new genetic variations. Thus, it is not surprising to see that, when new environmental challenges arise, species are able to adapt to them. More than two hundred insect and rodent species, for example, have developed resistance to the pesticide DDT in parts of the world where spraying has been intense. Although these animals had never before encountered this synthetic compound, they adapted to it by means of mutations that allowed them to survive in its presence and thus were rapidly multiplied by natural selection.

The resistance of disease-causing bacteria and parasites to antibiotics and other drugs is a consequence of the same process. When an individual receives an antibiotic that specifically kills the bacteria causing a disease—say, tuberculosis—the immense majority of the bacteria die, but one in a million may have a mutation that provides resistance to the antibiotic. These resistant bacteria will survive and multiply, and the antibiotic will no longer cure the disease. This is the reason why modern medicine treats bacterial diseases with cocktails of antibiotics. If the incidence of a mutation conferring resistance for a given antibiotic is one in a million, the incidence of one bacterium carrying three mutations, each conferring resistance to one of three antibiotics, is one in a quintillion (one followed by eighteen zeros); such bacteria are far less likely, if not altogether impossible, to exist in any infected individual.

Natural Selection "Creates" Novelty

Natural selection is sometimes perceived as a purely negative process, the elimination of harmful mutations. But natural selection is much more than that, for it is able to generate novelty by increasing the probability of otherwise extremely improbable genetic combinations. Natural selection is thus a creative process. It does not create the component entities upon which it operates (genetic mutations), but it produces adaptive combinations that could not have existed otherwise.

The combination of genetic units that carries the hereditary information responsible for the formation of the vertebrate eye could have never been produced purely by a random process—not even if we allow for the three and a half billion years during which life has existed on earth. This is the argument advanced by proponents of intelligent design. But evolution is not a process governed by random events. The complicated anatomy of the eye, like the exact functioning of the kidney, is the result of a nonrandom process—natural selection.

How natural selection, a purely natural process, can generate novelty in the form of accumulated hereditary information, by proceeding one step at a time, may be illustrated by the following example. Some strains of *Escherichia coli* (bacteria common in the colon of humans and other mammals and often used in laboratory experiments), in order to be able to reproduce in a laboratory culture, require that a certain substance, the amino acid histidine, be provided in the culture. When a few such bacteria are added to a small glass tube containing a liquid culture medium, they multiply rapidly and produce between twenty and thirty billion bacteria in one or two days. If a drop of the antibiotic streptomycin is added to the culture, most bacteria will die, but after a day or two the culture will again teem with billions of bacteria. Why?

Spontaneous genetic mutations to streptomycin resistance occur in normal (that is, nonresistant) bacteria at random, at rates of the order of one in one hundred million (1×10^{-8}) bacterial cells. In a bacterial culture with twenty to thirty billion bacteria, we expect between two hundred and three hundred bacteria to be resistant to streptomycin due to spontaneous mutation. When the antibiotic is added to the culture, only the resistant cells survive. The two or three hundred surviving bacteria will reproduce so that, after one or two days, twenty or so billion bacteria will be present, all resistant to streptomycin.

Consider now a second step in this experiment. The streptomycin-resistant cells are transferred to a culture with streptomycin but without histidine, an amino acid that they require in order to grow and reproduce. Most of the bacteria will fail to reproduce and will die, yet, after a day or two, the culture will be teeming with billions of bacteria. This is because among cells requiring histidine as a growth factor, spontaneous mutants able to reproduce in the absence of histidine spontaneously arise at rates of about four in one hundred million (4×10^{-8}) bacteria. If the culture has twenty to thirty billion bacteria, about one thousand bacteria will survive in the absence of histidine and will reproduce until the available culture medium is saturated.

Natural selection has produced, in two steps, bacterial cells resistant to streptomycin and not requiring histidine for growth. The probability of these two mutations happening in the same bacterium is about four in ten million billion ($1 \times 10^{-8} \times 4 \times 10^{-8} = 4 \times 10^{-16}$) cells. An event of such low probability is unlikely to occur even in a large laboratory culture of bacterial cells. With natural selection, cells having both properties are the common result. A "complex" trait made up of two components has come about by natural processes. It can readily be understood that the example can be extended to three, four, and more component steps. At the end of the long process of evolution, we have organisms each exhibiting features "designed" for their survival in the habitat where they happen to exist. Thus natural selection is a creative process, although it does not create the raw materials—the genes or DNA—upon which it acts.

Step by Step

Several hundred million generations separate modern animals from the early animals of the Cambrian geological period (542 million years ago). The number of mutations that can be tested, and those eventually selected, in millions of individual animals over millions of generations is hard to fathom for a human mind. But we can readily understand that the accumulation of millions of small, functionally advantageous changes could yield remarkably complex and adaptive organs, such as the eye.

The critical point is that evolution by natural selection is an incremental process, operating over time and yielding organisms better able to survive and reproduce than others, which typically differ from one another at any one time only in small ways; for example, the difference between having or lacking an enzyme able to synthesize histidine. It may be worth pointing out that increased complexity is not a necessary outcome of natural selection, although increases in complexity occur from time to time in evolution. Over time's eons, multitudes of complex organisms have arisen on earth.

Increased complexity is not a necessary consequence of natural selection but emerges occasionally as a matter of statistical bias. Occasionally, a mutation that increases complexity will be favored by natural selection, while other mutations will not increase complexity. Mutations that increase complexity will occasionally accumulate over time. A simple example is *Volvox*, a spherical multicellular organism with differentiated cells, some specialized for reproduction. Volvox differs from some unicellular algae (*Chlamydomona*) by only between three and five mutations.

The longest living organisms on earth are the microscopic bacteria, which have continuously existed on our planet for three and a half billion years and yet exhibit no greater complexity than their old-time ancestors. More complex organisms came about much later, without the elimination of their simpler relatives. For example, the primates appeared on earth only fifty million years ago, and our species, *Homo sapiens*, came about less than two hundred thousand years ago.

Natural selection produces combinations of genes that would otherwise be highly improbable because natural selection proceeds step by step, as illustrated by the bacterial example. The human eye did not appear suddenly in all its present perfection. Its formation required the appropriate integration of many genetic units. The eye could not have resulted from random processes alone, nor did it come about suddenly or in a few steps. Our ancestors had for more than half a billion years some kind of organs sensitive to light. Perception of light and, later, vision were important for these organisms' survival and reproductive success. Accordingly, natural selection favored genes and gene combinations increasing the functional efficiency of the eye. Such genetic units gradually accumulated, eventually leading to the highly complex and efficient vertebrate eye.

A record of the major stages in the evolution of the complex eye has survived in living mollusks (clams, snails, and squids). The eye of octopuses and squids is as complex as the human eye, with cornea, iris, refractive lens, retina, vitreous internal substance, optic nerve, and muscle. Limpets (*Patella*) have the simplest eye imaginable: just an eye spot consisting of a few pigmented cells with nerve fibers attached to them. Several intermediate stages are found in other living mollusks.

One step in complexity above the limpet eye is found in split-shell mollusks (*Pleurotomaria*), which have just a cup eye, one layer of pigmented cells curved like a cup with a wide opening through which light enters, with each pigmented cell attached to a nerve fiber. More complex is the pinhole-lens eye found in *Nautilus*, a marine snail. The layer of pigmented cells is considerably more extensive than in split-shell mollusks; the pigmented cells are covered toward the front with epithelium (skin) cells that are nearly closed except for a small opening ("pinhole") for passage of light, creating a cavity filled with water.

Murex, another marine snail, has an eye with a primitive, refractive lens covered with epithelium cells (serving as a primitive cornea); the pigmented cells extend through the back of the eye cavity (thus serving as a retina), and the nerve fibers are collected into an optic nerve that goes to the brain.

The most advanced mollusk eye is found in the octopus and the squid. It is just as complex and effective as the human eye and lacks the blind spot. The imperfection of the blind spot in the human eye is due to the fact that the nerve fibers of the human eye are collected inside the eye cavity, so that the optic nerve has to cross the retina on its way to the brain. By contrast, the nerve fibers and the optic nerve of the octopus eye are outside the eye cavity and travel to the brain without crossing the retina.[2]

Chance and Necessity

An engineer has a preconception of what he or she wants to design and will select suitable

materials and modify the design so that it fulfills
the intended function. On the contrary, natural
selection has no foresight, nor does it operate
according to some preconceived plan. Rather,
it is a purely natural process resulting from the
interacting properties of physicochemical and
biological entities. Natural selection is simply
a consequence of the differential survival and
reproduction of living beings. It has some appear-
ance of purposefulness because it is conditioned
by the environment: which organisms survive
and reproduce more effectively depends on which
variations they happen to possess that are useful
in the place and at the time the organisms live.

But natural selection does not anticipate the
environments of the future; drastic environmental
changes may be insuperable to organisms that were
previously thriving. Species extinction is a common outcome of the evolutionary process. The species existing today represent the balance between
the origin of new species and their eventual extinction. The available inventory of living species has
identified and described nearly two million species, although at least ten million are estimated to
be now in existence. But we know that more than
99 percent of all species that ever lived on earth
have become extinct without issue. Thus, since the
beginning of life on earth 3.5 billion years ago, the
number of different species that have lived on our
planet is likely to be more than one billion.

Adaptation to a given habitat may occur in
a variety of different ways. An example may be

taken from the adaptations of plant life to the desert climate. The fundamental adaptation is to the condition of dryness, which involves the danger of desiccation. During a major part of the year, sometimes for several years in succession, there is no rain. Plants have accomplished the urgent necessity of saving water in different ways. Cacti have transformed their leaves into spines, having made their stems into barrels storing a reserve of water; photosynthesis is performed on the surface of the stem instead of in the leaves. Other plants have no leaves during the dry season, but after it rains, they burst into leaves and flowers and quickly produce seeds. A third mode of adaptation is that of ephemeral plants, which germinate from seeds, grow, flower, and produce seeds—all within the space of the few weeks when rainwater is available; the rest of the year the seeds lie quiescent in the soil.

The opportunistic character of natural selection is also well evidenced by the phenomenon known as "adaptive radiation." As pointed out in chapter 4, each of the world's continents has its own distinctive collection of animals and plants. Certain animals occur in Africa but not in South America, and vice versa. In Australia, there is a great diversity of marsupial mammals, which lack placenta, so that much of early development takes place in a mother's external pouch, rather than inside the mother's womb. Marsupials include the kangaroos but also moles, anteaters, and Tasmanian wolfs.

These vagaries of biogeography are not due solely to the suitability of the different environments (see chapter 4). When rabbits were introduced in Australia (which, like other placental mammals, are not native to that continent), they prospered and became an agricultural pest. Hawaii lacks native land mammals, but feral pigs and goats introduced in the nineteenth century for hunting sports have multiplied so greatly that they are now endangering the native vegetation.

The vagaries of biogeography evince the opportunism of natural selection, which depends on past history, such as what organisms happened to colonize a territory, and on the occurrence of mutations and other chance events that open up certain evolutionary pathways and close others. Adaptive radiation, on a scale lesser than continental, is apparent in islands distant from large land masses. Darwin was startled by the Galapagos's tortoises, giant lizards, mockingbirds, and finches, different as they were from mainland species and diverse among the islands as well.

6

Intelligent Design

The argument from design (see chapter 2) was revived by several authors in the 1990s, notably William Dembski, Michael Behe, and Phillip Johnson,[1] among others. Often these authors sought to hide that their argument from design was an argument for the existence of God, so that intelligent design theory could be taught in the public schools, as an alternative to the theory of evolution, without incurring conflict with the United States Constitution, which forbids the endorsement of any religious beliefs in public institutions.

The folly of this pretense, namely that the intelligent design argument is scientific rather than religious, is apparent to anybody seriously considering the issue. As Judge John E. Jones writes in the *Dover* decision of December 20, 2005: "Although proponents of IDM [intelligent design movement] occasionally suggest that the designer could be a space alien or a time-traveling cell biologist, no serious alternative to God as a designer has been proposed by members of the IDM." Further, Professor Behe's

> testimony at trial indicated that ID is only a scientific, as opposed to a religious, project for him; however, considerable evidence was introduced to refute this claim. . . . ID's religious nature is evident because it involves a supernatural designer. . . . Expert witness ID proponents confirmed that the existence of a supernatural designer is a hallmark of ID.[2]

The duplicity of ID proponents concerning their religious objectives is particularly distressing, precisely because it is ostensibly adopted to further religion. "It is ironic," writes Judge Jones, "that several . . . individuals, who so staunchly and proudly touted their religious convictions in public, would time and again lie to cover their tracks and disguise the real purpose behind the ID policy."[3]

Acknowledging that ID is a religious argument does not make it invalid. It is to this issue of the cogency of ID that I now turn by considering various claims of ID proponents.

The "Theory" of Evolution

Opponents to teaching the theory of evolution in the public schools declare that it is only a "theory" and not a "fact." Indeed, they add, science relies on observation, replication, and experiment, but nobody has seen the origin of the universe or the evolution of species, nor have these events been replicated in the laboratory or by experiment.

When scientists talk about the "theory" of evolution, they use the word differently from how people use it in ordinary speech. In everyday speech, *theory* often means *guess* or *hunch*, as in "I have a theory as to why there were so many hurricanes in the year 2005." In science, however, a theory is a well-substantiated explanation of some aspect of the natural world that incorporates observations, facts, laws, inferences, and tested hypotheses. Scientists sometimes use the word *theory* for tentative explanations that lack substantial supporting evidence. Such tentative explanations are more accurately called *hypotheses*.

According to the theory of evolution, organisms are related by common descent. There is a multiplicity of species because organisms change from generation to generation, and different lineages change in different ways. Species that share a recent ancestor are therefore more similar than those with remote ancestors. Thus, humans and chimpanzees are, in configuration and genetic makeup, more similar to each other than they are to baboons or to elephants.

Scientists agree that the evolutionary origin of animals and plants is a scientific conclusion beyond reasonable doubt. They place it beside such established concepts as the roundness of the earth, its rotation around the sun, and the molecular composition of matter. That evolution has occurred, in other words, is a fact.

How is this factual claim compatible with the accepted view that science relies on observation, replication, and experimentation, even though nobody has observed the evolution of species, much less replicated it by experiment? What scientists observe are not the concepts or general conclusions of theories but their consequences. Copernicus's heliocentric theory affirms that the earth rotates around the sun. Nobody has observed this phenomenon, but we accept it because of numerous confirmations of its predicted consequences.

We accept that matter is made of atoms, even though nobody may have seen them, because of corroborating observations and experiments in physics and chemistry. The same is true of the theory of evolution. For example, the claim that humans and chimpanzees are more closely related to each other than they are to baboons leads to the prediction that the DNA is more similar between humans and chimps than between chimps and baboons. To test this prediction, scientists select a particular gene, examine its DNA structure in each species, and thus corroborate the inference. Experiments of this kind are replicated in a variety of ways to gain further confidence in the conclusion. And so it is for myriad predictions and inferences between all sorts of organisms.

Not every part of the theory of evolution is equally certain. Many aspects remain subject to research, discussion, and discovery. But uncertainty about these aspects does not cast doubt on the fact of evolution. Similarly, we do not know all the details about the configuration of the Rocky Mountains and how they came about, but this is not reason to doubt that the Rockies exist. Evolutionary biology is one of the most active fields of scientific research at present, and significant discoveries continually accumulate, supported in great part by advances in other biological disciplines.

The theory of evolution needs to be taught in the schools because nothing in biology makes sense without it. Modern biology has broken the genetic code, developed highly productive crops, and provided knowledge for improved health care. Students need to be properly trained in biology in order to deepen their education, develop appreciation for the natural world and their place in it, increase their chances for gainful employment, and enjoy a meaningful life in a technological world.

Learning about evolution has practical value. The theory of evolution has made important contributions to society. Evolution explains why many human pathogens have developed resistance to formerly effective drugs and suggests ways of confronting this increasingly serious problem. Evolutionary biology has also contributed importantly to agriculture by explaining the relationships among wild and domesticated plants and animals and their natural enemies. An understanding of evolution is indispensable in order to establish sustainable relationships with the natural environment.

Through a Glass Darkly

One frequent delusion of ID proponents asserts, implicitly or explicitly, that if evolution fails to explain some biological phenomenon, intelligent design must be the correct explanation. This is a misunderstanding of the scientific process. If one explanation fails, it does not necessarily follow that some other explanation is correct. Explanations must stand on their own evidence, not on the failure of their alternatives. Scientific explanations or hypotheses are creations of the mind, conjectures, imaginative exploits about the makeup and operations of the natural world. It is the imaginative preconception of what might be true in a particular case that guides observations and experiments designed to test whether the hypothesis is correct. The degree of acceptance of a hypothesis is related to the severity of the tests that it has passed.

The discovery of oxygen did not simply happen because it was shown that phlogiston does not exist. Nor is the periodic table of chemical elements accepted just because chemical substances react and yield a variety of components. Similarly, Darwin's theory of evolution by natural selection became generally accepted by scientists because it has sustained innumerable tests and has been fertile in yielding new knowledge. Other evolutionary theories, such as Lamarck's, have failed the tests of science. For a theory to be accepted, it is not sufficient for some alternative theory to have failed.

This point was forcefully made by Judge Jones in *Dover*:

> ID is at bottom premised upon a false dichotomy, namely that to the extent evolutionary theory is discredited, ID is confirmed. . . . The same argument . . . was employed by creationists in the 1980s to support "creation science." . . . The court in *McLean* [the Arkansas federal district decision of January 5, 1982] noted the "fallacious pedagogy of the two model approach" and that . . . "in support of creation science, the defendants relied upon the same false premise . . . all evidence which criticized evolutionary theory was proof in support of creation science." We do not find this false dichotomy any more availing to justify ID today than it was to justify creation science two decades ago.[4]

Irreducible Complexity?

The call for an intelligent designer is predicated by ID proponents on the existence of irreducible complexity in organisms. An irreducibly complex system is defined by Behe as being "composed of several well-matched, interacting parts that contribute to the basic function, wherein the removal of any one of the parts causes the system to effectively cease functioning." Intelligent-design proponents have argued that irreducibly complex systems cannot be the outcome of evolution.

According to Behe,

> An irreducibly complex system cannot be produced directly ... by slight, successive modifications of a precursor system, because any precursor to an irreducible complex system that is missing a part is by definition nonfunctional.... Since natural selection can only choose systems that are already working, then if a biological system cannot be produced gradually it would have to arise as an integrated unit, in one fell swoop, for natural selection to have anything to act on.[5]

In other words, unless all parts of the eye come simultaneously into existence, the eye cannot function; it does not benefit a precursor organism to have just a retina, or a lens, if the other parts are lacking. The human eye, according to this argument, could not have evolved one small step at a time, in the piecemeal manner by which natural selection works.

But evolutionists have pointed out, again and again, with supporting evidence, that organs and other components of living beings are not irreducibly complex—they do not come about suddenly, or in one fell swoop. Evolutionists have shown that the organs and systems claimed by intelligent-design theorists to be irreducibly complex—such as the eye (see chapter 6) or the bacterial flagellum (see below)—are not irreducible at all; rather, less complex versions of the same systems can be found in today's organisms.

The human eye did not appear suddenly in all its present complexity. Its formation required the integration of many genetic units, each improving the performance of preexisting, functionally less perfect eyes. About 700 million years ago, the ancestors of today's vertebrates already had light-sensitive organs. Mere perception of light and, later, various levels of vision were beneficial to these organisms living in environments pervaded by sunlight. Different kinds of eyes have independently evolved at least forty times in animals, which exhibit a full range of complexities and patterns. Sunlight is a pervasive feature of earth's environment; it is not surprising that organs have evolved that take advantage of it.

Some multicellular animals exhibit simple light-sensitive spots on their epidermis, as in the case of limpets (chapter 6). Further steps—deposition of pigment around the spot, configuration of cells into a cuplike shape, thickening of the epidermis leading to the development of a lens, development of muscles to move the eyes and nerves to transmit optical signals to the brain—gradually led to the highly developed eyes of vertebrates and cephalopods (octopuses and squids) and to the compound eyes of insects.

The gradual process of natural selection adapting organs to functions occurs in a variety of ways, reflecting the haphazard component of evolution due to mutation, past history, and the vagaries of environments. In some cases the changes of an organ amount to a shift of function, as in the evolution of the forelimbs of vertebrates, originally adapted for walking, which are used in birds for flying, in whales for swimming, and in humans for handling objects. Other cases, as the evolution of eyes, exemplify gradual advancement of the same function—such as seeing. In all cases, however, the process is impelled by natural selection's favoring through time individuals exhibiting functional advantages over others of the same species.

The Bacterial Flagellum and Other Improbabilities

A favorite example of alleged irreducible complexity is the bacterial flagellum. The bacterial flagellum is, according to Behe, irreducibly complex because it consists of several parts so that, if any part is missing, the flagellum will not function. It could not, therefore, says Behe, have evolved gradually, one part at a time, because the function belongs to the whole, the separate parts cannot function by themselves. "Because the bacterial flagellum is necessarily composed of at least three parts—a paddle, a rotor, and a motor—it is irreducibly complex."[6]

The flagellum is embedded in the cell membrane of the bacteria. The external swimming element that functions as paddle or propeller is a filament consisting of a single kind of protein, called *flagellin*. At the cell membrane, the filament attaches to a "rotor," made up of a so-called hook protein. The motor that rotates the filament is located at the base of the flagellum and consists of two elements: a rotor (the part that rotates) and a stator (the stationary component).

The argument that the different components of the flagellum must have come about "in one fell swoop," because the parts cannot function separately and thus could not have evolved independently, is reminiscent of Paley's argument (and Behe's) about the eye. Of what possible use would be the iris, cornea, lens, retina, and optic nerve, one without the others? Yet we know that component elements of the octopus eye can evolve gradually, cumulatively, and that simple eyes, as they exist in a limpet, in shell mollusks, and in marine snails, are functional.

The bacterial flagellum does not exist. In different species of bacteria there are different kinds of flagella, some simpler than the one described by Behe, others just different—even very different, as in the archaea, a very large group of bacteria-like organisms. Moreover, motility in many bacteria is accomplished without flagella at all. Biochemists have shown that some flagellum components may have evolved from secretory systems, which are very similar to the flagellum but lack some of the flagellum's components. The flagellum described by Behe has essentially the same structure as type-III secretory systems, although these lack the motor protein.

This small book is hardly the appropriate venue to enter into the technical details of how bacterial flagella may have evolved gradually, in some cases derived from structures originally evolved for different functions, such as secretion, nor the place to cite the scientific papers in which the technical details are given. General discussions can be found in the writings, for example, of Ian Musgrave, David Ussery, and Kenneth Miller.[7] Reviewing the matter, Miller points out that

> The most powerful rebuttals of the flagellum story, however, have not come from direct attempts to answer the critics of evolution. Rather, they have emerged from the steady progress of scientific work on the genes and proteins associated with the flagellum and other cellular structures. Such studies have now established that the entire premise by which this molecular machine has been advanced as an argument against evolution is wrong—the bacterial flagellum is not irreducibly complex.[8]

The process of blood coagulation is another example Behe has used as evidence of intelligent design. An injured person bleeds for a short time until a clot forms, which soon hardens, and the bleeding stops. As Behe writes, "Blood clotting is a very complex, intricately woven system consisting of a score of interdependent protein parts." Blood clotting is such a complex process and seemingly so unnecessarily complex that Behe has compared it to a machine designed by Rube Goldberg, the great cartoonist who designed very complex machines to perform tasks that could be accomplished much more simply. The coagulating mechanism is one of Behe's examples of intelligently designed bio-chemical processes. According to Behe, "*no one on earth has the vaguest idea how the coagulation cascade came to be*" (his italics).[9] This is a remarkable statement. Apparently, Behe is unaware of papers such as "The Evolution of Vertebrate Blood Coagulation" by the eminent biochemist Russell F. Doolittle, as well as numerous other publications by Doolittle and other scientists.[10]

Michael Behe has written that "there is no publication in the scientific literature—in prestigious journals, specialty journals, or books—that describes how molecular evolution of any real, complex, biochemical system either did occur or even might have occurred" and, in particular, "the scientific literature has no answers to the origin of the immune system."[11] In *Dover*, Judge Jones, points out with understated disbelief that

> Professor Behe was questioned concerning his 1996 claim that science would never find an evolutionary explanation for the immune system. He was presented with fifty-eight peer-reviewed publications, nine books, and several immunology textbook chapters about the evolution of the immune system; however, he simply insisted that this was still not sufficient evidence of evolution, and that it was not "good enough."

Judge Jones concluded, "We therefore find that Professor Behe's claim for irreducible complexity has been refuted in peer-reviewed research papers and has been rejected by the scientific community at large."[12]

William Dembski has written that irreducible complexity is a special case of "complex specified information," which is information that has a very low prior probability and therefore high information content. Dembski argues that mutation and natural selection are incapable of generating such highly improbable states of affairs.

Take the thirty proteins that make up the bacterial flagellum. Assuming that each protein has about three hundred amino acids, he calculates that the probability of one such protein is 20^{-300}. After some refinements, he calculates that the probability of origination for the flagellum is 10^{-1170} (1 divided by 1 followed by 1,170 zeros). Dembski concludes that even if life has existed on earth for three and a half billion years, the assembly of a functioning flagellum is impossibly improbable.

What is one to make of this calculation? The answer is simple: this calculation, as well as Dembski's other numerology exercises, is totally irrelevant, because Dembski's assumptions are wrong. Natural selection proceeding step-wise can accomplish outcomes with prior probabilities immensely smaller than Dembski's calculations. (The explanation can be found in chapter 5.) In the example given, the probability that one single bacterium would acquire resistance to the antibiotic streptomycin and the ability to synthesize the amino acid histidine is extremely small. Yet all twenty to thirty billion bacteria in the final culture exhibit these properties. They have been accomplished by natural selection in response to the environmental changes in just a few days.

Darwin's Gift

One difficulty with attributing the design of organisms to the Creator is that imperfections and defects pervade the living world. In the human eye, for example, the visual nerve fibers in the eye converge on an area of the retina to form the optic nerve and thus create a blind spot; squids and octopuses do not have this defect. Defective design would seem incompatible with an omnipotent intelligent designer.

Anticipating this criticism, Paley responded that "apparent blemishes . . . ought to be referred to some cause, though we be ignorant of it." Modern intelligent-design theorists have made similar assertions. According to Behe,

> the argument from imperfection overlooks the possibility that the designer might have multiple motives, with engineering excellence oftentimes relegated to a secondary role. . . . The reasons that a designer would or would not do anything are virtually impossible to know unless the designer tells you specifically what those reasons are.[13]

This statement, scientists and philosophers have responded, might have theological validity, but it destroys intelligent design as a scientific hypothesis, because it provides it with an empirically impenetrable shield against predictions of how "intelligent" or "perfect" a design will be. Science tests its hypotheses by observing whether or not predictions derived from them are the case in the observable world. A hypothesis that cannot be tested empirically—that is, by observation or experiment—is not scientific. Intelligent design as an explanation for the adaptations of organisms could be (natural) theology, as Paley would have it, but, whatever it is, it is not a scientific hypothesis.

The theory of intelligent design is not good theology either, because it leads to conclusions about the nature of the designer quite different from those of omniscience, omnipotence, and benevolence that Christian theology predicates of God. It is not only that organisms and their parts are less than perfect but also that deficiencies and dysfunctions are pervasive. Consider the human jaw. Because we have too many teeth for the jaw's size, wisdom teeth need to be removed, and orthodontists make a decent living straightening the others. Would we want to blame God for this blunder? A human engineer would have done better.

Evolution gives a good account of this imperfection. Brain size increased over time in our ancestors; the remodeling of the skull to fit the larger brain entailed a reduction of the jaw, so that the head of the newborn would not be too large to pass through the mother's birth canal. Evolution responds to the organisms' needs through natural selection not by optimal design but by "tinkering," by slowly modifying existing structures. Evolution achieves "design" as a consequence of natural selection while promoting adaptation. Evolution is "imperfect" design, rather than intelligent design.

Consider the birth canal of women, much too narrow for easy passage of the infant's head, so that thousands upon thousands of babies and many mothers die during delivery. Surely we don't want to blame God for this dysfunctional design or for the children's deaths. Science makes it understandable, a consequence of the evolutionary enlargement of our brain. Females of other primates do not experience this difficulty. Theologians in the past struggled with the issue of dysfunction because they thought it had to be attributed to God's design. Science, much to the relief of many theologians, provides an explanation that convincingly attributes defects, deformities, and dysfunctions to natural causes.

Examples of deficiencies and dysfunctions in all sorts of organisms can be endlessly multiplied, reflecting the opportunistic, tinkerer-like character of natural selection. The world of organisms also abounds in characteristics that might be called "oddities," as well as those that have been characterized as "cruelties," an apposite qualifier if the cruel behaviors were designed outcomes of a being holding on to human or higher standards of morality. But the cruelties of biological nature are only metaphorical cruelties when applied to the outcomes of natural selection.

Examples of "cruelty" involve not only the actions of predators (say, a chimpanzee) tearing apart their prey (say, a small monkey held alive and screaming by a chimpanzee biting large flesh morsels from it) or parasites destroying the functional organs of their hosts but also, and very abundantly, interactions between organisms of the same species, including between mates. A well-known example is the female praying mantis, which devours the male after coitus is completed. Less familiar is the fact that, if she gets the opportunity, the female will eat the head of the male *before* mating; thrashing the headless male mantis into spasms of "sexual frenzy" allows the female to connect his genitalia with hers.[14]

In some midges (tiny flies), the female captures the male as if he were any other prey and with the tip of her proboscis she injects her spittle into his head. Her spittle starts digesting the male's innards, which are then sucked by the female; partly protected from digestion are the relatively intact male organs, which break off inside the female and fertilize her.[15]

Cannibalism is known in dozens of species, particularly spiders and scorpions. The world of life abounds in "cruel" behaviors. Numerous predators eat their prey alive; parasites destroy their living hosts from within; in many species of spiders and insects, the females devour their mates.

The design of organisms is often so dysfunctional, odd, or cruel that it possibly could be attributed to the gods of the ancient Greeks, Romans, and Egyptians, who fought with one another, made blunders, and were clumsy in their endeavors. But for a modern biologist who knows about the world of life, the design of organisms is not compatible with special action by the omniscient and omnipotent God of Judaism, Christianity, and Islam.

Religious scholars in the past struggled with imperfection, dysfunction, and cruelty in the living world, finding them difficult to explain as the outcome of God's design. Evolution, in one respect, came to their rescue. Jack Haught, a contemporary Roman Catholic theologian, has written of "Darwin's gift to theology."[16] The Protestant theologian Arthur Peacocke has referred to Darwin as the "disguised friend," by quoting the earlier theologian Aubrey Moore, who wrote in 1891: "Darwinism appeared, and, under the guise of a foe, did the work of a friend."[17] Peacocke acknowledges the irony that the theory of evolution, which at first had seemed to remove the need for God in the world, now has convincingly removed the need to explain the world's imperfections as outcomes of God's design.

7

Belief

I want to make in this final chapter two main points, which to me seem obvious or, at least, beyond reasonable doubt. One point is that the theory of evolution is not incompatible with belief in the existence of God and God's presence in the workings of the universe. The second point is that science is a powerful and successful way of acquiring knowledge about the universe, but it is not the only way: other valid ways of acquiring knowledge about the universe include imaginative literature and other forms of art, common sense, philosophy, and religion. Some readers will surely disagree with one or both points, but I shall argue them as forcefully as I can, though briefly.

Curiously, the presupposition that the theory of evolution is incompatible with religious beliefs is shared by ID proponents (and other creationists) and materialistic scientists and philosophers. By contrast, I agree with Judge Jones in his *Dover* decision: "Many of the leading proponents of ID make a bedrock assumption which is utterly false.

Their presupposition is that evolutionary theory is antithetical to a belief in the existence of a supreme being and to religion in general."[1]

Evolution and the Bible

I will, first, briefly review the history of Christianity's response to the theory of evolution and the history of the creationism movement in the United States. The conclusion that I wish to draw out is that scientific knowledge and religious belief, if they are correctly assessed, *cannot* be in contradiction, because science and religion concern nonoverlapping realms of knowledge. It is only when assertions are made beyond their legitimate boundaries that evolutionary theory and religious belief appear to be antithetical.

Some Christians see the theory of evolution as incompatible with their religious beliefs because it contradicts the Bible's narrative of creation. The first chapters of Genesis describe God's creation of the world, plants, animals, and human beings. A literal interpretation of Genesis seems incompatible with the gradual evolution of humans and other organisms by natural processes. Independent of the biblical narrative, belief in the immortality of the soul and in humans as "created in the image of God" appear to many as contrary to the evolutionary origin of humans from nonhuman animals.

Religiously motivated attacks against the theory of evolution started during Darwin's lifetime. In 1874, Charles Hodge, an American Protestant theologian, published *What Is Darwinism?* one of the most articulate assaults on evolutionary theory. Hodge perceived Darwin's theory as "the most thoroughly naturalistic [and atheistic] that can be imagined." Echoing Paley, Hodge argued that the design of the human eye evinces that "it has been planned by the Creator, like the design of a watch evinces a watchmaker." He concluded that "the denial of design in nature is actually the denial of God."[2]

Other Protestant theologians saw a solution to the apparent contradiction between evolution and creation in the argument that God operates through intermediate causes. The origin and motion of the planets can be explained by the law of gravity and other natural processes without denying God's creation and providence. Similarly, evolution can be seen as the natural process through which God brought living beings into existence and developed them according to his plan. Thus, A. H. Strong, president of Rochester Theological Seminary in New York State, wrote in his *Systematic Theology* (1907): "We grant the principle of evolution, but we regard it as only the method of divine intelligence." Strong uses an analogy to argue that the brutish ancestry of human beings is not incompatible with their status as creatures in the image of God: "The wine in the miracle [Christ's miraculous conversion of water into wine] was not water because water had been used in the making of it, nor is man a brute because the brute has made some contributions to its creation."[3] Arguments for and against Darwin's theory came from Roman Catholics as well.

Gradually, well into the twentieth century, evolution by natural selection came to be accepted by a majority of Christian writers. Moreover, Pope Pius XII in his 1950 encyclical *Humani generis* ("Of the Human Race") acknowledged that biological evolution was compatible with the Christian faith, although he argued that God's intervention was necessary for the creation of the human soul. Pope John Paul II, in an address to the Pontifical Academy of Sciences on October 22, 1996, deplored interpreting the Bible's texts as scientific statements rather than religious teachings, adding:

New scientific knowledge has led us to realize that the theory of evolution is no longer a mere hypothesis. It is indeed remarkable that this theory has been progressively accepted by researchers, following a series of discoveries in various fields of knowledge. The convergence, neither sought nor fabricated, of the results of work that was conducted independently is in itself a significant argument in favor of this theory.[4]

Similar views have been expressed by other mainstream Christian denominations. The General Assembly of the United Presbyterian Church in 1982 adopted a resolution stating that "Biblical scholars and theological schools . . . find that the scientific theory of evolution does not conflict with their interpretation of the origins of life found in Biblical literature."[5] The Lutheran World Federation in 1965 affirmed that "evolution's assumptions are as much around us as the air we breathe and no more escapable. At the same time theology's affirmations are being made as responsibly as ever. In this sense both science and religion are here to stay, and . . . need to remain in a healthful tension of respect toward one another."[6]

Comparable statements have been advanced by Jewish authorities and those of other major religions. In 1984, the 95th Annual Convention of the Central Conference of American Rabbis adopted a resolution that stated: "Whereas the principles and concepts of biological evolution are basic to understanding science . . . we call upon science teachers and local school authorities in all states to demand quality textbooks that are based on modern, scientific knowledge and that exclude 'scientific' creationism."[7]

Opposing these views are Christian denominations that continue to endorse a so-called literal interpretation of the Bible. A succinct expression of this interpretation is found in the Statement of Belief of the Creation Research Society, founded in 1963 as a "professional organization of trained scientists and interested laypersons who are firmly committed to scientific special creation": "The Bible is the Written Word of God, and because it is inspired throughout, all of its assertions are historically and scientifically true in the original autographs. To the student of nature this means that the account of origins in Genesis is a factual presentation of simple historical truths."[8]

Many Bible scholars and theologians have long rejected a literal interpretation as untenable, however, because the Bible contains incompatible statements. The very beginning of Genesis presents two different creation narratives. Extending through chapter 1 and the first verses of chapter 2 is the familiar six-day narrative, in which God creates human beings—both "male and female"—in his own image on the sixth day, after creating light, earth, firmament, fish, fowl, and cattle. But in verse 4 of chapter 2 a different narrative starts, in which God creates a male human, then plants a garden and creates the animals, and only then proceeds to take a rib from the man to make a woman.

Which one of the two narratives is in error? The answer is: neither one; both are correct as religious narratives. Biblical scholars point out that the Bible is inerrant with respect to religious truth, not in matters that are of no significance to salvation. Augustine wrote in his *De Genesi ad litteram* ("Literal Commentary on Genesis"):

> It is also frequently asked what our belief must be about the form and shape of heaven, according to Sacred Scripture. . . . Such subjects are of no profit for those who seek beatitude. . . . In the matter of the shape of heaven, the sacred writers did not wish to teach men facts that could be of no avail for their salvation.[9]

Augustine is saying that Genesis is not an elementary book of astronomy. It is a book about religion, and it is not the purpose of its authors to settle questions about the shape of the universe that are of no relevance whatsoever for seeking salvation.

In the same vein, Pope John Paul II said in 1981:

> The Bible itself speaks to us of the origin of the universe and its make-up, not in order to provide us with a scientific treatise but in order to state the correct relationships of man with God and with the universe. Sacred Scripture wishes simply to declare that the world was created by God, and in order to teach this truth it expresses itself in the terms of the cosmology in use at the time of the writer. Any other teaching about the origin and make-up of the universe is alien to the intentions of the Bible, which does not wish to teach how the heavens were made but how one goes to heaven.[10]

John Paul's argument was clearly a response to Christian fundamentalists who see in Genesis a literal description of how the world was created by God.

Creationism and the Courts

In modern times, biblical fundamentalists have periodically gained considerable public and

political influence. Opposition to the teaching
of evolution can largely be traced to two movements with nineteenth-century roots, Seventh-
day Adventism and Pentecostalism.

Consistent with their emphasis on the seventh-day Sabbath as a memorial of the biblical
creation, Seventh-day Adventists have insisted on
the recent creation of life and the universality of
the biblical Flood, which they believe deposited
fossil-bearing rocks. This distinctively Adventist
interpretation of Genesis became the hard core of
"creation science" in the late twentieth century and
was incorporated into the "balanced treatment"
laws of Arkansas and Louisiana (see below).

Many Pentecostals, who generally subscribe
to a literal interpretation of the Bible, also have
adopted and endorsed the tenets of creation science,
including the recent origin of the earth and a geology interpreted in terms of the Flood. They differ
from Seventh-day Adventists and other adherents
of creation science, however, in their tolerance of
diverse views and the limited import they attribute
to the evolution-creation controversy.

During the 1920s, biblical fundamentalists
helped influence more than twenty state legislatures
to debate anti-evolution laws, and four states—
Arkansas, Mississippi, Oklahoma, and Tennessee—
prohibited the teaching of evolution in their public
schools. A spokesman for the anti-evolutionists,
William Jennings Bryan, three times the unsuccess-
ful Democratic candidate for the U.S. presidency,
said in 1922, "We will drive Darwinism from our

schools." In 1925, Bryan took part in the prosecution of John T. Scopes, a high school teacher in Dayton, Tennessee, who had violated the state's law forbidding the teaching of evolution.

In 1968, the Supreme Court of the United States declared unconstitutional any law banning the teaching of evolution in public schools. Thereafter, Christian fundamentalists introduced bills in a number of state legislatures ordering that the teaching of "evolution science" be balanced by allocating equal time to "creation science." Creation science, it was asserted, propounds that all kinds of organisms abruptly came into existence when God created the universe; that the world is only a few thousand years old; and that the biblical Flood was an actual event survived by only one pair of each animal species. In the 1980s, Arkansas and Louisiana passed acts requiring the balanced treatment of evolution science and creation science in their schools.

The Arkansas statute was declared unconstitutional in federal court after a public trial in Little Rock. The Louisiana law was appealed all the way to the Supreme Court of the United States, which in 1987 ruled Louisiana's "Creationism Act" unconstitutional because, by advancing the religious belief that a supernatural being created humankind—embraced by the phrase *creation science*—the act impermissibly endorses religion.

The most recent confrontation between creationism and the theory of evolution in the courts of law involves the concept of intelligent design, which in its current formulation came into existence after the Supreme Court's 1987 decision.

On October 28, 2004, the Dover (Pennsylvania) Area School Board of Directors adopted the following resolution: "Students will be made aware of gaps/problems in Darwin's theory and of other theories of evolution including, but not limited to, intelligent design." Further, on November 19, 2004, the Dover Area School District announced by press release that teachers would be required to read a statement, which includes the following assertions: "Because Darwin's Theory is a theory, it continues to be tested as new evidence is discovered. The Theory is not a fact. . . . Intelligent Design is an explanation of the origin of life that differs from Darwin's view."

The constitutional validity of the resolution and press release was challenged on December 14, 2004, in federal district court. On December 20, 2005, Judge John E. Jones III issued a 139-page decision (*Kitzmiller v. Dover Area School District*), declaring that "the Defendants' ID Policy violates the Establishment Clause of the First Amendment of the Constitution of the United States."[11]

Judge Jones reviewed the history of the creationist and ID movements in the United States and affirmed that "the overwhelming evidence at trial established that ID is a religious view, a mere re-labeling of creationism, and not a scientific theory"; "ID is not supported by any peer-reviewed research, data, or publications"; "it has not generated peer-reviewed publications, nor has it been the subject of testing and research"; "ID is not science and cannot be adjudged a valid, accepted scientific theory."[12]

Whether or not *Dover* will be appealed in the courts remains to be seen. In any case, fundamentalist creationism's efforts to discredit the theory of evolution will surely persist.

Science and Religious Beliefs

Is science fundamentally materialistic? Does Darwinism exclude religious beliefs? The answer to the second question is no. The answer to the first question is: It depends on whether one refers to scientific scope and methodology or to metaphysical conceits.

The scope of science is the world of nature, the reality that is observed, directly or indirectly, by our senses. Science advances explanations concerning the natural world, explanations that are subject to the possibility of corroboration or rejection by observation and experiment. Outside that world, science has no authority, no statements to make, no business whatsoever taking one position or another. Science has nothing decisive to say about values, whether economic, esthetic, or moral; about the meaning of life or its purpose; about religious beliefs as such.

Science is *methodologically* materialistic or, better, methodologically *naturalistic*. I prefer the second expression because "materialism" often refers to a metaphysical conception of the world, a philosophy that asserts that nothing exists beyond the world of matter, that nothing exists beyond what our senses can experience. That is why the question whether or not science is inherently naturalistic depends on whether we are referring to the methods and scope of science, which remain within the world of nature, or to the metaphysical implications of materialistic philosophy's assertion that nothing exists beyond the world of matter. Science does not imply metaphysical materialism.

Methodological naturalism asserts the boundaries of scientific knowledge, not its universality. Science transcends cultural, political, and religious differences because it has no assertions to make about these subjects as such. That science is not constrained by cultural or religious differences is one of its great virtues. But science does not transcend those differences by denying them or by taking one position rather than another. It transcends cultural, political, and religious differences because these matters are not its business.

Yet some scientists, including evolutionists, assert that science denies any valid knowledge concerning values or the world's meaning and purpose. The well-known evolutionist Richard Dawkins explicitly denies design, purpose, and values: "the universe that we observe has precisely the properties we should expect if there is, at bottom, no design, no purpose, no evil and no good, nothing but blind, pitiless indifference."[13] The historian of science William Provine not only affirms that there are no absolute principles of any sort, but draws the ultimate conclusion from this line of thinking that even free will is an illusion: "Modern science directly implies that there are no inherent moral or ethical laws, no absolute guiding principles for human society. . . . Free will as it is traditionally conceived. . . . simply does not exist."[14]

There is a monumental contradiction in these assertions. If its commitment to naturalism does not allow science to derive values, meaning, or purpose from scientific knowledge, it surely does not allow it to deny their existence. We may grant Dawkins and Provine their right to think as they wish, but they have no warrant whatsoever to ground their materialistic philosophy in the accomplishments of science. It is ironic that these authors are, in fact, endorsing the beliefs of ID proponents who argue that science is inherently materialist and share the ID conceit that science makes assertions about values, meaning, and purpose.

I will add something that seems obvious to me but becomes at times clouded by the hubris of some scientists. Successful as it is, and universally encompassing as its subject is, a scientific view of the world is hopelessly incomplete. Matters of value and meaning are outside science's scope. Scientific knowledge may enrich esthetic and moral perceptions and illuminate the significance of life and the world, but these are matters outside science's realm.

The National Academy of Sciences has asserted:

Religions and science answer different questions about the world. Whether there is a purpose to the universe or a purpose for human existence are not questions for science. . . . Consequently, many people, including many scientists, hold strong religious beliefs and simultaneously accept the occurrence of evolution.[15]

Scientific knowledge cannot contradict religious beliefs because science has nothing to say for or against revelation, religious realities, or religious values.

The National Academy of Sciences also asserts: "Within the Judeo-Christian religions, many people believe that God works through the process of evolution. That is, God has created both a world that is ever-changing and a mechanism through which creatures can adapt to environmental change over time."[16] The biologist Kenneth R. Miller, the Catholic theologian John F. Haught, the Episcopalian biochemist and theologian Arthur Peacocke, and so many other theologians and religious authors believe, indeed, that God works through the process of evolution.[17]

Augustine asserted that all things depend on God but they also depend, in a different sense, on their own immediate or distant created causes. "Augustine, too, tried to endow the world of created causes with a specific reality of its own, one distinct from the causal activity of God in the world."[18]

Some Christians, however, see the theory of evolution and scientific cosmology as contrary to the biblical story of creation. These believers are entitled, of course, to hold such convictions based on their interpretation of Scripture. But I will aver that Genesis is a book of religious revelations and religious teachings, not a treatise of astronomy or biology. Those who maintain that the Bible should be taken literally, in its religious teachings as well as in all historical and descriptive references to the world, encounter, as I have pointed out earlier, an insurmountable difficulty in the contradictory statements found in the Bible, such as the two inconsistent creation narratives in Genesis, or the erroneous statements about the sun's circling around the earth and the like.

I will, thus, bring this book to an end by reiterating the simple message with which I started it: It is possible to believe that God created the world while also accepting that the planets, mountains, plants, and animals came about, after the initial creation, by natural processes. Truth cannot go against truth. Religious believers should see in the magnificent achievements of modern science a manifestation of the glory of God, not a threat to their faith.

Acknowledgments

This book was prompted by an inquiry from Michael West, editor-in-chief, Fortress Press. He asked me to consider crafting a short book for intelligent lay persons, explaining the role and status of evolutionary theory . . . and how that contrasts with the assertions and status of the intelligent design proponents. I am grateful to Mr. West for this request and for his support, cooperation, and enthusiasm in following up with the project. I have also promised to the editors of the Joseph Henry Press (JHP) of the National Academy of Sciences that I would write a book on the same subject, although directed to a different audience. I am grateful as well to the principals of the Joseph Henry Press, who also agreed that both projects were compatible: Barbara Kline Pope, Stephen Mautner, and Jeffrey Robbins. *Darwin's Gift* is the intended title for the JHP book.

I am grateful to Abby Hartman, production editor, Fortress Press, and to Beth Wright, for their thoughtful editing of the manuscript and for numerous courtesies. My debt to Denise Chilcote for preparing the manuscript is very extensive and so is my gratitude. As my executive assistant for nineteen years, she has never failed to do whatever needed to be done as well as it could be done. I have tremendously benefited from her dedication and perfectionism.

Notes

Chapter 1

1. Augustine, *The City of God against the Pagans*, ed. and trans. R. W. Dyson, Cambridge Texts in the History of Political Thought (Cambridge: Cambridge University Press, 1998), 452–53, cited in Michael Ruse, "The Argument from Design," in *Debating Design: From Darwin to DNA*, ed. William A. Dembski and Michael Ruse (Cambridge: Cambridge University Press, 2004), 13–31.

2. Thomas Aquinas, *Summa Theologica, Part I*, trans. by the author (London: Burns, Oates, Washbourne, 1952), 27.

3. John Ray, *The Wisdom of God, Manifested in the Works of Creation* (London, 1691), 33.

4. William Paley, *Natural Theology* (New York: American Tract Society, n.d.), 22. This American edition is undated but seems to have been printed in the late nineteenth century.

5. Ibid., 48.

6. Ibid.

7. Ibid., 1.

8. Ibid.

9. Ibid., 175–76.

10. Ibid., 47.

11. Ibid., 46.

12. See Michael Roberts, "Intelligent Design: Some Geological, Historical, and Theological Questions," in Dembski and Ruse, eds., *Debating Design*, 282.

13. As quoted by George Gaylord Simpson, *This View of Life: The World of an Evolutionist* (New York: Harcourt, Brace & World, 1964), 192.

Chapter 2

1. Charles Darwin, *Charles Darwin's Autobiography*, ed. Sir Francis Darwin, Life of Science Library (New York: Schuman, 1961), 34–35.

2. Charles Darwin, *On the Origin of Species* (New York: Atheneum, 1967 [1859]), 489–90; emphasis added.

3. Ibid., 490; emphasis added.

4. In his autobiography Darwin wrote, "The old argument of design in nature, as given by Paley, which formerly seemed to me so conclusive, falls, now that the law of natural selection has been discovered. We can no longer argue that, for instance, the beautiful hinge of a bivalve shell must have been made by an intelligent being, like the hinge of a door by a man." *The Autobiography of Charles Darwin, 1809–1882: With Original Omissions Restored*, ed. Nora Barlow (London: Collins, 1958).

5. See chapter 3 in Niles Eldredge, *Darwin* (New York: Norton, 2005), 71–138, for a review of the Red and Transmutation B to E Notebooks.

6. Wallace's essay was published in the *Journal of the Proceedings of the Linnean Society of London (Zoology)* 3 (1858): 53–62.

7. Ibid., 53.

8. *Origin*, note 2 above, 306.

Chapter 3

1. This assumption, later called the inheritance of acquired characteristics (or Lamarckism), was disproved

in the twentieth century.

2. Phylum (plural = phyla) is the category below kingdom and above class in the biological taxonomy of living things. The lowest, or most specific, categories are genus and species.

3. Edward B. Daeschler, Neil H. Shubin, and Farish A. Jenkins Jr., "A Devonian Tetrapod-Like Fish and the Evolution of the Tetrapod Body Plan," *Nature* 440 (2006): 757–63; Neil H. Shubin, Edward B. Daeschler, and Farish A. Jenkins Jr., "The Pectoral Fin of *Tiktaalik roseae* and the Origin of the Tetrapod Limb," *Nature* 440 (2006): 764–71.

4. Gerald Mayr, Burkhard Pohl, and D. Stefan Peters, "A Well-Preserved *Archaeopteryx* Specimen with Theropod Features," *Science* 310 (2005): 1483–86.

5. DNA (deoxyribonucleic acid) is a double-helix molecule that contains the genetic instructions for building proteins. (See the section in chapter 5 "Mutations and DNA" for an overview of the structure of DNA.) For an excellent introduction to the basics of DNA (in the context of human biology), visit http://learn.genetics. utah.edu/units/basics/tour.

Chapter 4

1. Tim D. White et al., "Asa Issie, Aramis and the Origin of *Australopithecus*," *Nature* 440 (2006): 883–89.

Chapter 5

1. Charles Darwin, *On the Origin of Species* (New York: Atheneum, 1967 [1859]), 80–81.

2. A figure representing the five examples of mollusk eyes that I have described can be seen in figure 13 of "Evolution, The Theory of," *Encyclopaedia Britannica* (2005), 18:855–91.

Chapter 6

1. William A. Dembski, *The Design Inference: Eliminating Chance through Small Probabilities*, Cambridge Studies in Probability, Induction and Decision Theory (Cambridge: Cambridge University Press, 1998); Michael J. Behe, *Darwin's Black Box: The Biochemical Challenge to Evolution* (New York: Free Press, 1996); Phillip E. Johnson, *The Wedge of Truth: Splitting the Foundations of Naturalism* (Downers Grove, IL: InterVarsity Press, 2000).

2. John E. Jones III, *Kitzmiller v. Dover Area School District*, December 20, 2005, 25, 28–29.

3. Ibid., 137,

4. Ibid., 71.

5. Behe, *Darwin's Black Box*, 39.

6. Ibid., 72.

7. Ian Musgrave, "Evolution of the Bacterial Flagellum," in *Why Intelligent Design Fails: A Scientific Critique of the New Creationism*, ed. Matt Young and Taner Edis (New Brunswick, NJ: Rutgers University Press, 2004), 72–84; David Ussery, "Darwin's Transparent Box: The Biochemical Evidence for Evolution," in Young and Edis, eds., *Why Intelligent Design Fails*, 48–57.

8. Kenneth Miller, "The Flagellum Unspun: The Collapse of 'Irreducible Complexity,'" in *Debating Design: From Darwin to DNA*, ed. William A. Dembski and Michael Ruse (Cambridge: Cambridge University Press, 2004), 81–97.

9. Behe, *Darwin's Black Box*, 78, 97.

10. R. S. Doolittle, "The Evolution of Vertebrate Blood-Coagulation—A Case of Yin and Yang," *Thrombosis and Haemostasis* 70 (1993): 24–28. See references and discussion in David J. Depew and Bruce H. Weber, "Darwinism, Design, and Complex Systems Dynamics," in Dembski and Ruse, eds., *Debating Design*, 173–90; Niall Shanks and Istvan Karsai, "Self-Organization and the Origin of Complexity," in Young and Edis, eds., *Why Intelligent Design Fails*, 85–106; Miller, "The Flagellum Unspun."

11. Behe, *Darwin's Black Box*, 185, 138.

12. Jones, *Kitzmiller v. Dover Area School District*, 78–79.

13. Behe, *Darwin's Black Box*, 223.

14. S. E. Lawrence, "Sexual Cannibalism in the Praying Mantis, *Mantis religiosa*: A Field Study," *Animal Behaviour* 43 (1992): 569–83; see also M. A. Elgar, "Sexual Cannibalism in Spiders and Other Invertebrates," in *Cannibalism: Ecology and Evolution among Diverse Taxa*, ed. Mark A. Elgar and Bernard J. Crespi (Oxford: Oxford University Press, 1992).

15. J. A. Downes, "Feeding and Mating in the Insectivorous Ceratopogoninae (Diptera)," *Memoirs of the Entomological Society of Canada* 104 (1978): 1–62. Diverse sorts of oddities associated with mating behavior are described in the delightful as well as accurate and documented book by Olivia Judson, *Dr. Tatiana's Sex Advice to All Creation* (New York: Holt, 2002).

16. Jack Haught, "Darwin's Gift to Theology," in *Evolutionary and Molecular Biology: Scientific Perspectives on Divine Action*, ed. Robert John Russell, William R. Stoeger, and Francisco J. Ayala (Vatican City State: Vatican Observatory; Berkeley: Center for Theology and the Natural Sciences, 1998), 393–418.

17. Arthur Peacocke, "Biological Evolution—A Positive Appraisal," in Russell, Stoeger, and Ayala, eds., *Evolutionary and Molecular Biology*, 357–76.

Chapter 7

1. See previous chapter, note 2.

2. Charles Hodge, *What Is Darwinism?* (New York: Scribner, Armstrong & Co., 1874), 85, 60, 173.

3. A. H. Strong, *Systematic Theology*, 3 vols. (Westwood, NJ: Fleming Revell, 1907), 2:473, 472.

4. John Paul II, address to the Pontifical Academy of Sciences, October 22, 1996. Original French text published in *L'Osservatore Romano*, October 23, 1996. English

edition published in *L'Osservatore Romano*, October 30, 1996. Both texts are reproduced in R. J. Russell, W. R. Stoeger, and F. J. Ayala, eds., *Evolutionary and Molecular Biology: Scientific Perspectives on Divine Action* (Vatican City State: Vatican Observatory; Berkeley: Center for Theology and the Natural Sciences, 1998), 2-9.

5. General Assembly of the United Presbyterian Church, 1982), Molleen Matsumura, ed., *Voices for Evolution* (Berkeley, CA: National Center for Science Education, revised edition, 1995), 107.

6. Ibid., 96.

7. Ibid., 88.

8. E. C. Scott, *Evolution vs. Creationism* (Westport, CT: Greenwood Press, 2004), 100.

9. St. Augustine, *The Literal Meaning of Genesis (De Genesi ad Litteram)*, book 2, chapter 9. There are several translations of this book into English: see, for example, the edition "Translated and Annotated by John Hammond Taylor, S.J., 2 volumes (New York: Newman Press, 1982), vol. 1, 58-59.

10. John Paul II, address to the Pontifical Academy of Sciences on October 3, 1981, cited in Matsumura, note 4 above, 97.

11. John E. Jones III, *Kitzmiller v. Dover Area School District*, December 20, 2005, 139.

12. Ibid., 43, 87, 64, 89.

13. Richard Dawkins, *River Out of Eden: A Darwinian View of Life* (New York: Harper Collins, 1992), 133.

14. William Provine, "Evolution and the Foundation of Ethics," *MBL Science* 3 (1988): 25-29.

15. National Academy of Sciences, *Teaching about Evolution and the Nature of Science* (Washington, DC: National Academy Press, 1998), 58.

16. Ibid.

17. Kenneth R. Miller, *Finding Darwin's God: A Scientist's Search for Common Ground between God and Evolution* (New York: Cliff Street Books, 1999); John Haught, "Darwin, Design, and Divine Providence,"

in *Debating Design: From Darwin to DNA*, ed. William A. Dembski and Michael Ruse (Cambridge: Cambridge University Press, 2004), 229–45; Arthur Peacocke, "Biological Evolution—A Positive Appraisal," in *Evolutionary and Molecular Biology: Scientific Perspectives on Divine Action*, ed. Robert John Russell, William R. Stoeger, and Francisco J. Ayala (Vatican City State: Vatican Observatory; Berkeley: Center for Theology and the Natural Sciences, 1998).

18. R. A. Markus, "Augustine, St.," in *The Encyclopedia of Philosophy*, 2 vols. (New York: Macmillan, 1972 [1967]), 1:205.

Additional Resources

There are numerous books thoughtfully dealing with the perceived conflict between evolution and religion. I recommend the following:

Dembski, William A., and Michael Ruse, eds. *Debating Design: From Darwin to DNA* (Cambridge: Cambridge University Press, 2004).

Miller, Kenneth R. *Finding Darwin's God: A Scientist's Search for Common Ground between God and Evolution* (New York: Harper Collins, 1999).

Moore, John A. *From Genesis to Genetics: The Case of Evolution and Creationism* (Berkeley: University of California Press, 2002).

Pennock, Robert T. *Tower of Babel: The Evidence against the New Creationism* (Cambridge, Mass.: MIT Press, 2002).

Peters, Ted, and Marty Hewlett. *Can You Believe in God and Evolution? A Guide for the Perplexed* (Nashville: Abingdon, 2006).

Scott, Eugenie C. *Evolution vs. Creationism: An Introduction* (Westport, Conn.: Greenwood, 2004).

Young, Matt, and Taner Edis, eds. *Why Intelligent Design Fails: A Scientific Critique of the New Creationism* (New Brunswick, N.J.: Rutgers University Press, 2004).

The following two documents are relatively brief, very readable, and authoritative. (I chaired the committee that drafted Science and Creationism.*)*

National Academy of Sciences. *Science and Creationism: A View from the National Academy of Sciences,* Second Edition (Washington, D.C.: National Academy Press, 1999).

National Academy of Sciences. *Teaching about Evolution and the Nature of Science* (Washington, D.C.: National Academy Press, 1998).

A good source for religious, scientific, educational, and civic statements in support of evolution is:

Matsumura, Molleen, ed. *Voices for Evolution* (Berkeley, Calif.: The National Center for Science Education, 1995).

Excellent books that explore general issues concerning science from a religious perspective and vice versa are:

Haught, John F. *Science and Religion: From Conflict to Conversation* (New York: Paulist Press, 1995).

Lindberg, David C., and Ronald L. Numbers, eds. *God and Nature: Historical Essays on the Encounter between Christianity and Science* (Berkeley: University of California Press, 1986).

Numbers, Ronald L. *Darwinism Comes to America* (Cambridge, MA: Harvard University Press, 1998).

Peters, Ted, and Martinez Hewlett. *Evolution from Creation to New Creation: Conflict, Conversation, and Convergence* (Nashville: Albingdon, 2003).

Ruse, Michael. *Can a Darwinian Be a Christian? The Relationship between Science and Religion* (Cambridge: Cambridge University Press, 2001).

Russell, Robert John, William R. Stoeger, and Francisco J. Ayala, eds. *Evolutionary and Molecular Biology:*

Scientific Perspectives on Divine Action (Vatican City State/Berkeley, California: Vatican Observatory and the Center for Theology and the Natural Sciences, 1998).